To J4

The Sharpest Tool to Wealth

How Your WORDS Create Your WORLD

By

Esperanza Montalvo

With love & wealth

Esperanza.

THE SHARPEST TOOL TO WEALTH
Copyright 2010 by ESPERANZA MONTALVO

All rights reserved. No part of this book may be used or reproduced in any manner whatsoever without written permission from ESPERANZA MONTALVO, except as provided by the United States of America copyright law or in the case of brief quotations embodied in articles and reviews.
The scanning, uploading and distribution of this book via the Internet or via any other means without the permission of the publisher is illegal and punishable by law.

Please purchase only authorized electronic editions and do not participate in or encourage electronic piracy of copyrighted materials. Your support of the author's rights is sincerely appreciated.

Printed in the United States of America.

First Printing: 2010

Dedication

To my son Jimmy, his wife Jodi, and my three beautiful grandchildren, Amalia, Cruz E. & Mateo for being a fountain of unconditional love, support, and joy in my life. You are an extraordinary anchor to my purpose, and I love you very much.

Acknowledgements

Many pages could be filled with the amazing people who supported and encouraged me through the process of completing this book. At this time, I want to acknowledge and thank:

- *My Son Jimmy for the Book Cover Picture and his creative ideas throughout the writing of this book. Your unconditional support is limitless. Thank you.*

- *My sister Gloria and brother in-law David who constantly encouraged me to write a book. They put a seed in my heart, and thanks to their constant reminders, here it is. Some topics are derived from our yearly Dialogues. Thank you.*

- *My family: my sisters and brothers (and spouses) who are always by my side, with graceful encouragement and understanding. Gloria & David, Javier & Milena, Ruby, Marta & Richard, Beatriz & Jacques. My nephews and niece (spouses & family) for being such incredible cheerleaders in my life: Hernan & Rachelle, Juan Felipe & Andrea, Lina Maria; and cousin Gloria - To all of you, thank you for your support.*

- *All my Toastmasters colleagues and friends who have listened to my speeches throughout the years.*

- *Special thanks to my Editor, Mitchell Parent, who questioned me fearlessly for clarity. Your sharp awareness and wit will be forever appreciated.*

- *Ann McIndoo, my Author's Coach, who got this book out of my head and into your hands. It is a true joy to work with you, Ann.*

Contents

SESSION III: TALKING TO GOD / YOUR HIGHER SELF

SESSION IV: TALKING TO MONEY

Foreword

The author of this book subscribes to the view of those who believe that we have entered into a new reality as a result of the New Paradigm. Nowadays, it is not age, social background and status, cultural heritage, education, physical appearance, or the past that determines our success (that is the old paradigm) – but living our purpose and passion every day of our lives. We are seeing far-reaching changes in the global economy. We are seeing propitious changes in the accountability of leadership even within closed-minded societies. We are experiencing new appreciation for global diversity and family values as never before. And we presume that beneficent technologies and widespread, virtually instant communication have a lot to do with these global changes.

The ideas presented in this book are intended for human beings who are prepared to accept that Wealth is much more than being "money-rich" and that being truly wealthy entails having a balance between our Spiritual, Mental, Emotional and Physical worlds. The ideas in this book challenge readers to rise above their years, their cultural background and their social conditioning. They are intended to stimulate readers to view themselves and others from a broader perspective as a means of promoting human betterment.

Four chapters are provided in this book. The first Chapter, "How to Talk to Ourselves", examines the consequences of our Self-Talk and the importance of discovering it and bringing it into our conscious awareness. Making the conscious choice to transform it, so as to get different results, is up to us. As you read this chapter, you will experience the urgency to explore and become aware of your present 'Self-Talk'.

The second topic, "How to Talk to Others", focuses on the fact that the greatest resource in our lives is "Other People".   In order to create the relationships that are enriching and expanding to 'one and other', this chapter shows you concepts, methods and ways of achieving such a connection – one where everyone is empowered.

The third Chapter, "How to Talk to God", is an expansion of the two previous ones depending on how you know your God. Speaking about balance, the author asserts that when our communication is disconnected from our greatest power (some call it God), our results do not amount to what we are capable of creating. When this communication does not exist, we miss the opportunity to use all of our human potential. This Chapter encompasses the ways in which we can elevate our human consciousness and communicate with the Infinite Consciousness – that which has all the answers.

The fourth Chapter, "How to Talk to Money", explores the ways toward breaking the old assumptions about money. It explains how to open up to receiving the infinite Wealth that surrounds us after we gain a new awareness of 'How we talk to Ourselves, How we talk to Others, and How we talk to God'.

A few years ago, the author and I undertook once-a-week Dialogue sessions for a year or more. On these occasions, we created the opportunity to explore and inquire into a variety of the topics presented in this book. Although our discussions explored some spiritual, poetic and traditional aspects of these topics, the author has augmented and transformed these into a guideline for practical application. It is with pleasure that I write this Foreword and recommend the book to the prospective reader.

--David Gadd, Ph.D.

"A Note from the Author"
The Power of Words

The Blind Beggar and the Journalist

There was a blind beggar sitting on a busy street with a bowl and a small board, on which some words were written in black marker.

They read:

I'm blind. Please help Me!

A creative journalist who passed by noticed the few coins and bills in the beggar's bowl. Without asking the beggar's permission, the journalist picked-up the piece of board, turned it around, and with a black marker he wrote another message.

He put the piece of board by the blind beggar's feet and left. In the afternoon, he passed by the beggar again. Her bowl was filled with coins and bills.

The blind beggar, recognizing his walk, asked the journalist if he was the one who wrote on her piece of board, and more importantly, what was it that <u>he wrote</u>.

The Journalist answered: Nothing as true as your message but with **different Words**. He smiled and continued on his way.

The new message said:

Today is spring and I can't see it!

Change your strategy when something is not working, and you'll see different results – what needs to change, it can be as simple as the Words you are using.

No one can be a slave of his or her identity.   When there is an opportunity for change, we must change.

The most dangerous human beings are those who have been injected with fear—The Fear of Change.

If you do what you've always done
You will get what you've always got.

Discover the Dialogues of your Life
to Discover your WEALTH SWITCH

Introduction

When we want to arrive somewhere we've never been before, what do we need in order to get there?

- A **Destination** – an address
- A **Vehicle** to get there
- A **Map** or GPS
- **To be Focused** on the road
- **Awareness**
- **Persistence** to face any challenge
- The **Attitude** of **Certainty** that the specific place will be reached

So it is with our life!

As any recipe needs to have all the ingredients to taste exactly as it was planned, so it is with any destination we choose to experience in our lives—We can choose to experience in the moment, or we can choose to experience in the future. What do you prefer?

*It is the **WORDS** we use
that bring any experience we desire into the
realm of the **Now**—The only plane where
anything **exists**.*

For years I had forgotten the Power of Words and the manifesting force they had. As a child, I was not a talker, in fact, many people considered me to be a very quiet and shy little girl—I had gone through years of introspection and observation. Deep down I had this awareness that words were like seeds, and that the fresh minds of children were being filled with the words spoken by parents, teachers, those in authority who shape their lives. This awareness disappeared during my teenage and young adult years, until I began my university studies where I realized that most of what I knew intuitively had been said by others.

My search for awareness began in Canada when I first got to see Mark Victor Hansen in one of his presentations about Love—by the time I got to the office that day, I was transformed from the inside out.   After that experience, I immersed myself in personal development and personal growth, which is now recognized by companies, organizations, institutions to be a basis for professional development. In reality, they cannot be separated as one is the other.

I have developed Corporate Training Seminars based on the philosophy that "Companies Don't Succeed, People Do!"

What does this mean? It is not the building or the systems that makes a company succeed, but the people in it. When I first understood this, I literally jumped with joy, because I knew that whether or not you are called a professional, you are always a "person" first. As such, all of us have values to live by, dreams to realize, visions to complete, purposes to fulfill, challenges to face, and so on.

As I realized that yes, we have all these complexities in our lives, there had to be something that those who achieved the results I wanted were doing. When I began seeing the results my Words were producing, I knew that something had to change. A decision came about to do something drastic. I wanted to go for the **cause and not the consequence**. I knew deep down that fixing the results was not the answer. Something deeper needed to change, and it wasn't others, it wasn't the circumstances, it was something within me.

What was I asking for? Or NOT asking for? How did I describe myself? What did I say to myself when something didn't go the way I planned? What did I say about others? How did I connect with people? When did I create strong relationships? What took place? Did I know how to hear the voice of God? Did I pay attention to my inner voice? Did I know it existed? How about money? How did I talk to money? Did I even talk to money? Or did I ignore it?

As you can see, I went through a serious analysis of the words I was using and the results they were producing. I made alarming discoveries during this process, and my efforts were then dedicated to putting everything I knew and learned into action so that I could then, later on, share with the world the results of my life experiences. Each of us has a story to share with the world—put it into words.

Back to my topic—It has been my experience throughout my personal and professional development that as I share this concept with more and more people, and they apply it, the results show almost immediately.

What does it take? It takes your desire to welcome the ideas expressed in this book, and your **decision** to make them your own, what

17

will ultimately produce the results you are looking for. I can share hundreds of examples of clients who have come to me and said, "If only I knew this before".

This is your opportunity to become inspired; and to apply some of the ideas presented here in this book to your life. And to go a little further with them: share them with others, because as we share we learn, as we teach we learn, and as we contribute, we succeed.

*My intention is that you will become passionately conscious about the **WORDS** you use, and become mindful and observant of the RESULTS they can produce.*

To your Wealth,

Esperanza Montalvo, International Speaker & Coach
2010

Session I: Talking to Ourselves

Chapter One
Our Words Our World

What Defines Us?

Our lives, our reality, our world is defined by both our Inner and Outer world. Our thoughts, beliefs, attitudes, and conditioning as well as our environment, experiences, social structures, the books we read, the people we grow up with, everything, influence who we are at a specific time in our lives.

The visible, or what we get to see in others, is a small part compared to what it's underneath the visible behaviors. As in the iceberg, where the top is only one small part of it, so it is with people. There's much more than what we can see with our naked eyes.

Who we are and what defines us is NOT the same. We can change our definitions as easily as we can change our stories. We have the power to do this when we re-write our stories using different descriptions, different words. As we rewrite our stories, we create a mental paradigm that will guide us towards new experiences - whatever it is we choose to experience. Sometimes we keep ourselves in a position where we want to relive our past. We try to hold on to our history. The past is the past; it is gone; it only exists in our mind. If it doesn't serve a purpose, let it go; if there is a reason for it, embrace it. We can choose, create, and experience a new life. And it's all our own decision.

I clearly remember the day I decided to be a writer. It was a conscious decision made with precision and clarity. Circumstances began to organize in support of my decision. Quintessentially, there were challenges, fears, doubts I encountered along the way, and being aware of them, I used whatever resource I had available to overcome them--these enemies of creativity. See more on tools to overcome the enemies of creativity @ www.thesharpesttooltowealth.com.

What Forces Build Our Language?

As we are faced with new experiences we need to learn the lingo that goes with them in order to belong and connect. When we are children we learn to express our immediate needs, as we grow older we learn to express our feelings, as we continue to grow we develop our ability to solve problems, make decisions, create dreams, build our vision, and design our destiny. All of these forces motivate us to learn a new language, learn new words, change our manner of speech, and ultimately, decide how we want our life to be.

While studying Communications at the University of Calgary I clearly remember the first time I wrote a paper on 'women and language'. It was then I discovered how our language creates our social structures, and how we are, more culturally designed by our language than by our genetics. Having lived and studied in Canada since my early adulthood, as opposed to other members of my family, I was able to distinguish clearly how the way I spoke and communicated was so different from those who had stayed in Colombia, my country of origin—there were many clashes given the differences— the value of asking questions to clarify, of respecting the opinions of others, of tolerating different points of views, of being able to disagree without fear of rejection, to hold a conversation without judgment and many other aspects, created an opportunity for me to study the differences. In fact, because of my involvement with clients from all over the world, I realized each culture and language have their own intrinsic rules. Because of this experience, I learned to be more tolerant and understanding with my communication.

When the differences become clear to us, it becomes easier to dissolve arguments and deal with conflict. For example, I had a Russian student who sounded as though he was really angry. It wasn't that he was angry, but that linguistic qualities of his language carry a tone that it was stronger than either English or Spanish.

Wealth and Words – How Do They Relate?

Have you heard the expression, "a Wealth of Words?" It is not a coincidence that this is one of those sayings that has been used throughout generations. There is wisdom in the combination of these two words. Even phonetically, the words rhyme, but better yet, the image that they both convey is one of infinite expansion. They seem to dance together for some inexplicable reason.

What have you been told? Were you told that you could be powerful and successful, or, were you told the opposite? A little note to some women – If you didn't hear the words "powerful" and "successful"as you were growing up, simply observe what took place, then, let it go. Now, choose to begin talking with assertiveness, certainty, and precision about what you want to be, do, and have in this order. When I speak of 'Wealth' I refer to well-being in all aspects of our lives—including spiritual, mental, emotional and physical—regarding the physical, it took me a while to embrace the word 'money' and its energy. There will be more on this subject under the session 'Talking to Money'.

Since wealth is connected to our words we need to look at our inconsistencies when we speak. Is what we say congruent with what we think? Is how we act congruent with what we want? I encourage you, from now on, to pay attention, consciously, fully, to what you're creating with your words. This is a call for you to take your words seriously.

Why Should It Matter?

Much of the separation that exists between our inner and outer worlds happens because of misinterpretation, lack of awareness and, **not knowing** the complexity of the World of Words. It is the conscious decision to look into the powerful World of Words that makes the difference.

The Unknown Factor

Let me tell you what I've called the "Unknown Factor" which blocks many of us at different times. Interestingly enough, this factor (UF) is one of the most dangerous saboteurs of our Wealth, or Freedom or Success (you choose whichever word you'd like to refer to). Experience has shown that 'what we don't know, we fear'. Have you ever found yourself saying "No" to something you haven't even tried? One of our first reactions towards the unknown is to say no to it—It is safe. It stops us from taking risks, from failing, from being ridiculed, from not being perfect. What will happen when we break free from the walls that create our fear of the unknown? Using your sharpest tool, your words, begin picturing yourself, in your mind and with your words, as energy flowing freely towards possibilities. As it is set free, it attracts only that which is focused on the energy of a specific time. No past and no future come into the picture, only the present and what we desire to focus on.

When I made the decision to focus on wealth and speak it into existence, what came about was only Wealth. My perception is painted by my words, my perception is my reality, and therefore, my words are my reality.

EXERCISE

Step #1 - Choose one 'value' to focus on for a day –

- o **Harmony** – that your relationships will be based on understanding

- o **Compassion** – that you can hear the needs of others without judgment

- o **Unconditional love** – that you accept others with their fears, doubts, ambitions, dreams, etc.

o **Humor** – that you can laugh at events even those that are challenging

o **Generosity** – that you can give openly of your time, money and yourself

o **Peace** – that nothing will disturb you as you accept the 'what is'

o **Money** – that you know you are provided and Source is abundant

o **Forgiveness** – that you **can** change your perspective and forgive yourself first

o **Other** – choose your own

Step #2 - Write down your experience for the day as you focus on a specific value.

What took place?

What did you find out during this day?

What questions came up? What obstacles did you face?

What was new or revealing to you?

What new questions do you have?

What then , and then, and then.

Step #3 - Share your experience with the people who support you throughout your journey. As we share, we deepen our awareness and contribute to the awareness of others.

When Is the Time to Wake Up?

The time is NOW! Waking up to having a relationship with your Words because they matter, is a transformational step in your life. It is not the Past, it is not the Future, but the Present, that brings you into the new World you so much desire.

What inspired you to buy this book? Something within the title and description prompted you to take the first step. I've always said that it takes a second for our consciousness to reveal a glimpse of what we need to do. It is us who take the action and began building upon that discovery. Be aware that once you take step one, it is only down hill trip. The right people begin to show up, the right books fall into your lap; synchronicities begin to appear in your life, and the question is, is this right for me now? Yes. You've already made the decision in your mind, now start speaking and claiming it. Remember, there's power in your words, and this power no one can take away from you. Cherish it as you would cherish anything important to you. What value would you put on it? The more value you give it, the more powerful it will become.

If Not Our Words, Then What?

Can you imagine having a resource available to you 24/7? When you fully believe the power that you have in your words, you will be in state of gratitude every second of your life. If a gift is something that is receive out of kindness, your words are the greatest gift you have been given. One of the first books I read, during my personal development journey was "Hung by the Tongue" by Francis F. Martin , which explains (biblically) the Power of our Words. This little book planted a seed in me that grew daily to the extent that people would say to me, "You are going overboard." And when others began seeing my results, they stopped condemning me and instead asked me how to do it, so I began to teach.

This is the time for me to share with you the process that takes place when you begin transforming or doing something you've never done before:

Be aware that:

- ❖ Others (some) will reject your new way of being and doing.

- ❖ Take any and all rejections as a compliment. See it as your compass indicating that you are changing.

- ❖ Continue in the direction of your vision—in other words, put on the blinders so that you don't become distracted.

- ❖ Begin experiencing how others will either catch up with what you're doing or leave you. That's Ok.

We attract those who vibrate at same level of energy or the level we desire. Once our vibration changes, so do our associations and relationships – it is the Law of Vibration in action.

Words That Changed the World

Many have been the words that have created new paradigms, new ways of thinking, new perceptions, new realities. Remember the speech, "I have a dream" by Martin Luther King? Who can forget these powerful words? Did they not create a new world? And when we think about it, the transformation that came about happened just because someone had the guts to put his vision into words and express it to the world. Can words change the world? Absolutely.

> "Gandhi had no armies at his command,
> and yet he mobilized tens of millions,
> and his words still do so today."

Susan B. Anthony, on women's right to vote said: *"Women are people, and thus, should have the same rights as men."* Her words greatly inspired her followers and helped keep the dream alive.

Nelson Mandela in his inaugural address spoke words of determination, patience and forgiveness. His words are words that will forever inspire, "We shall build a society in which all South Africans, both black and white, will be able to walk tall …"

No doubt there are many impacting words spoken by others, and many others to come - Words spoken with power are heard, served as inspiration, and cause history to change.

To be reminded of the Power of Words, we only have to read the biographies of people who have made a difference in this world. It often starts with a Vision, put into Words.

It was late February when I was talking to a lady who can hear the voice of intuition very clearly. That morning, as we were having breakfast, she said to me, "I heard a message that said, "Speak to Diana". Who walks into the room? Diana. Immediately I asked her how she could hear that voice so clearly, "I feel it instead of hear it", I said to her. All she said to me was, "**Begin** *saying,* "I hear the voice." Sure enough, later on, I heard the message. What did she actually tell me? To say the word I wanted to bring to my consciousness. She didn't even know I was writing a book about this concept.

How does this work? We need to know in our hearts that it works. That's all it takes. Make the decision to believe it and know it. I always want to bring you back to the power of Words. She said, "Began saying, "I hear." All it took was to change the word 'feel' to 'hear'. Is it magic? I'd like to say yes.

I happen to be surrounded by many people who take this concept to heart. Last night I was talking to my friend Myrta, and in my conversation I used the word 'should'. Immediately she said to me, "Say 'could' or 'choose' instead." You see, the word 'should' brings the factor of guilt into the picture. The word 'should' takes our power away. Instead, the word 'could' or 'choose' give our power back—It implies that I had a choice in the matter—that I consciously knew I could have done it differently. There is no condemnation in the words 'could or choose'. Some of you might say that this is taking words literality, to an extreme. If you are asking this question, stop, and look at your results. When someone says to me, "That's extreme," or "You take things too seriously," my next question is, "How is your way working for you?"

In one of the Communication Programs I deliver to corporations, there is a session where we study words and sentences that take away the power of a presenter or speaker. Why do you think I teach this in corporations? What do corporations look for? Employees who produce positive results. If our purpose is to get to our destination; if our purpose is to produce the results we are looking for; if our purpose is to be on point, then having the resources and tools to get us there and using them is the answer. If we know this, and decide not to do it, what would our results be?

Just look at the EQUATION :

Our Words = Our Results

Put any word to the left and get a result equivalent to that.
Fearful words = fearful results
Optimistic words = optimistic results
Creative words = creative results

Don't just believe what I'm saying, think about it. Try it yourself and see the transformation in your life.

There is a new movement that began with WORDS of a vision for the future; "Awaken the Dreamer's Dream." This is about a new world. The vision began with Words spoken so that others be inspired to act upon them.

In fact, every accomplishment has been put into WORDS in order to create an image in the mind of humanity.

What kind of images do we create in our minds with the words we use?

Do we create images of fear or images of Light, and Life? Do we create images of hope, or images of despair? Do we create images of success, or failure? Do we create images of Freedom, or Prison? What makes the difference is the words we use to create the images.

Take a look at this phrase: Are you in Prison or are you Free? What do these words convey? Can you feel it in your bones? I can. Words have the power to create feelings. How do you feel when you say, "I am overwhelmed" as opposed to saying, "I am excited"? How does your body respond?

Feelings prompt us to Act.
Feelings are created by our Words,
therefore, our *Words* prompt our *Actions*.

It is an axiom that we can look at it logically or intuitively, whatever moves you.

Words Inspire

Have you ever received a word that has helped you change the direction of your life? Or have you ever heard someone saying, "My high school teacher said something that changed my life and made me who I am today."

So words have the power to inspire; to make waves in the lives of others. We can inspire others to change their perspective and see things differently. We can actually inspire others, directly or indirectly, to change their mental attitude, and therefore act differently

Words are not to be taken lightly.

I've dedicated many years of my adulthood studying the essence of Words, and have had the opportunity to experience their Power. Philosophers, metaphysicists, Physicists have demonstrated that <u>when one thing in our life changes, everything changes.</u> If you don't like the results you're getting in your life, change your Vocabulary.

I used to use a lot of words of fear. I picked up this Fear vocabulary during my childhood. I was afraid of elevators, thunder, flying, heights, dark, you name it. Boy, was I afraid.

One day, I made a decision to conquer my fears. One of my first jobs in Canada was on the 51st floor of the tallest building in

Calgary (Canada) at that time. I knew right away that I had been put there for a reason, and on my way to facing my fear I had to find the tools to change.

I would get into the elevator, and knowing the power of words (affirmations), I would go all the way to the 51st floor repeating sentences such as: "I enjoy this elevator, I feel fantastic in high places, I can see from the top, I enjoy being high and having a high vision, etc. etc.". I had to convince myself, with words, that everything was OK. It worked. I began enjoying the ride and my fear disappeared.

I faced my fears little by little, and if it wasn't for the Words I filled my mind with, I'm not sure I had been able to conquer the phobias I had for so many years.

> Change your Vocabulary and your Mental Attitude will change.

Words have the power to change our lives, and because I began changing the dialogues of my life I discovered my Wealth Switch.

Chapter Two
Living In the World of Darkness

What's a Matter With You?

At times, *we* might be asking ourselves: "What's a matter with me?" Nothing is a matter. It is only that at times our perceptions are somewhat obscured by that world we don't get to see all the time. You might know what I'm talking about – I'm referring to that world that many have called the Subconscious; that world that gets filled with the words and ideas of our parents, teachers, environment, culture— all the forces that operate around us.

Scientifically explained, what others visibly see of our behavior it's only a small part of who we are. The observable behaviors and our mannerisms, that is, our visible reactions, are like the tip of an iceberg (approx. 25%). However, the deeper part of ourselves which contains our rules of conduct, feelings, doubts, fears, ambitions, dreams, attitudes, values, aspects that are unique to each of us and that are expressed intrinsically, is what others can only guess if we don't reveal to them. Thus, the expression, "I don't know you enough". What does it take to get to know the other and understand where they come from? Just imagine what it takes to explore approximately 75% of someone's make-up. Here is where the words we use play a big part on the development of our relationships.

The Iceberg

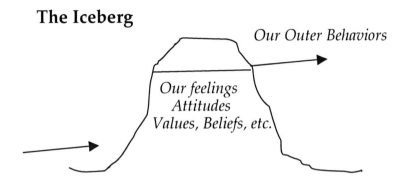

Our Outer Behaviors

*Our feelings
Attitudes
Values, Beliefs, etc.*

Where Does This Road Take Me?

When we operate on automatic, that is, without awareness and attention to what we are being, doing, and saying, the results will 'kindly' show us what we are creating. As Lewis Carroll wrote in Alice and Wonderland : *If you don't know where you are going, any road will get you there.* Do you want a compass? Get to know the power of your words and how it can take you to the road you desire.

Have you been with someone who repeatedly uses sarcastic vocabulary? Or a person who can only speak jokingly most of the time? Or one who refers to anything using jargon that you don't understand? How do these communication styles make you feel? The better question is, how do you communicate most of the time? What style do you use?

When we look carefully at our conversations and equate them with our relationships, we find that, "Our conversation = our relationship". And based on our conversations will our relationships be. For example, if my conversations are honest, so will be my relationship. If my conversation is authentic, so will be my relationship. If my conversation is filled with lies, so will my relationship be; and so on. You see the pattern.

In other words, whatever language we use in our conversations will directly affect the outcome of our relationships. We cannot expect apples from a pear tree, that is, we cannot expect our relationship to be any different from the words we use during our conversations.

Take this time to reflect on those conversations that seem to fill you up with energy, enthusiasm, hope, harmony—remember the words that flow during these exchanges. Similarly, go back to a conversation that filled you with anger, disappointment, and frustration. Explore the words that were exchanged, and notice the difference. What road do you want to take? You choose, and you can choose it with your Words.

Is There Light At the End of the Tunnel?

Wouldn't it be great to have a flashlight with us as we travel and journey through our lives? What if we can build a bright road as we walk together through this path we call life? Our moments of light can be created by ourselves. Our decision is in our words.

As I was waiting for my flight to California for a convention, a lady approached me to tell me that I reminded her of someone she knew. She immediately picked up that I spoke Spanish so we began our conversation. Mireya was from Panama and as a Registered Nurse, she has contact with people from all kinds of walks of life. When she found out about my book "How your words create your world" she proceeded to tell me how she strongly believed the same and how she lived her life under the same premise. "I spoke my life to existence," she said to me. How so? Was my next question, "Well, when I was young, I wanted to leave my country because I felt the need for freedom. In my mind, I thought the best way to do that was to marry an American and go and live in the States." Sure enough. She wrote her desire to marry someone from the USA and three weeks later she was in front of exactly what she was looking for. With a smile in her face, she then said to me, "And I got married two months later." How did this happen? I asked. "I only know that what I say is what I get when I say it with true intention, clarity and no doubt." She went on telling me how her grandma used to tell her to use her words as *commands*, and that as she experienced positive results, she would build her confidence.

"My life is a true representation of what your book is all about," she confirmed. Was I happy to hear this from someone I had just met? Of course. I mentioned I was going to use our short encounter in my book to which she gladly agreed.

I can see how some of you might be saying, "But I've done the same thing and nothing seems to happen. What is it? What am I doing wrong?" Let me assure you that you cannot do anything wrong. That you need more examples and experiences to deepen your awareness as to how this whole process works.

Whatever Happened?

Did we forget something? It seems that some of us forgot who we truly are and need to find our way back to our true nature.

Is there a tool, a vehicle, a path that can take us right back home? Certainly. Many theories have been exposed throughout the centuries. How about rekindling the simple and most readily available tool to us – The Power of our Tongue – the Power of Our Words!

What Then?

As we awaken to the realization that there is a permanent tool with us (Our Words) to create our world, and that the only need is to put it to work, we are on the road from Darkness to Freedom, or from Darkness to Wealth – which is the same as Freedom.

There is Power within us, but we need to ignite it. The Fuse is our Words! It sounds simple but we still have to put the action into effect. When we make our Words "verbs," or as my friend Sam put it, "commands," we ignite the dynamite, the Power that is within us. Some of us have given our Power to others as a means of feeling loved and as a mean of protecting ourselves from rejection. Some have given their Power away hoping that others will take care of them. Others out of fear of responsibility; and others, have simply done it from fear of being magnificent. It's incredible that we could fear being Magnificent. Marianne Williamson said, "Our deepest fear is not that we are inadequate; our deepest fear is that we are powerful beyond measure." When we stop to see where we are, and take the time to really look at who we really are, we begin our road back to freedom and Wealth. Our human potential is hidden behind all the mud we have covered it with throughout the years. It is then our job to work back or to go deep so we can rediscover that potentiality that is there, perhaps untapped, perhaps dormant, perhaps unknown to us. Many of my clients know me for describing human beings as "diamonds"—some of us need more cleaning than others, and others say we do not need so much cleaning, but true awareness of our diamond within, coupled with the courage to start living from this place of pure light.

Only If You Can Accept It

A gift needs to be accepted. When is not, it becomes a burden. How many times have you given a gift to someone who did not appreciate it? Do you feel like giving them one again? Something that is not appreciated is not given again. Take good care and use of your Words because it was a gift given to you.

Gratitude is the antidote of worry; how appropriate it is to bring gratitude at this moment in the book when we are in the process of moving from darkness to light. Holding two thoughts at the same time is impossible for human beings. Holding the thought of gratitude and its energy can only bring us to a higher level of consciousness. Being thankful for everything and anything removes worry out of our minds. Begin the morning with "I am grateful, I am alive, I am grateful I get to open my eyes, I am grateful I get to eat", and so on. End your day by being thankful for what you achieved, be grateful and even for your challenges or frustrations because they are always contributing to your expansion and growth. There are abundant reasons to be in a state of gratitude. Cultivate this habit and miracles begin to show up in your life. What is the role of our words in being grateful? They are the outcome of our inner state. Shout gratitude! Never be shy or tight with the expression of this amazing virtue. Use colorful words, feeling words, descriptive words, "*I feel grateful because of the radiant sun shinning upon me. I feel grateful because of the morning rain falling gently in my face. I am grateful because of the little baby's smile warming my heart.* I am grateful because I am alive this day"

Charged With the Energy of Fear?

Are your words producing fear or love? Words can have this kind of effect. What do you want in your life? Did you know that the words have energy? There is a meta-meaning (not explicit) that gives words energy, and as a result words could cause war or peace. Let's examine the energy surrounding our language and the outcome of such energy in our lives.

I had just finished facilitating training on personalities, perceptions and communication, when I came across this sentence: ***perspective is the antidote of fear.*** When we get to understand that everyone is entitled to their own perspective and that our perspective is our reality, we avoid a lot of miscommunication and conflict with others. When we want to make our point of view the only right point of view, what tends to create is much discord in our communication, and therefore our relationships.

During my language training classes for example, I often get participants from all over the world including China, Russia, Morocco, Sudan, Ethiopia, Mexico, Kosovo, Korea, Greece, Iran, Colombia, etc. In fact, I had a room once with students from 27 nationalities. Do they have different perspectives? Absolutely. Would one point of view be more 'correct' than other when it comes to talking about topics, often controversial? Do some actually *get scared* listening to the personal opinions of completely opposite views? Yes. Some do -- All this takes place in a classroom where people come from different religious, political and social backgrounds -- The art here is to create the attitude of 'I want to know how you think', which in reality means 'I want to show you the respect you deserve as a human being'. When this takes place, fear disappears.

Chapter Three
Hunger for Transformation

Abundance Is For Everyone

Abundance or scarcity is in the power of your tongue, and when it is said that abundance is for everyone; that means ALL with no exceptions. The only exception to this truism is your own limiting beliefs. The universe is limitlessly abundant, so enjoying its abundance is only up to you.

To live this type of consciousness requires that we leave behind our fears of the unknown, our fears of rejection, our fears of being transparent, our fears of being separate. Only when we align ourselves with the true essence of who we are, can we live in the abundance consciousness. The words we use define the consciousness we want to live in.

One of my clients said to me one day, "These are my rules and these rules I live by". When she told me her rules, I said to her, "Listen to the words you use to describe your rules. They are aligned with who you *show* me to be. I've known you for a couple of years and I could clearly see how the words you use to describe yourself reflect exactly how you portray yourself to others". How is that working for you?

When I said that, she looked at me with a smile in her face because deep down she knew her "true self" was not what she was describing. She had put a number of labels on herself, perhaps even put in there by others. Not having the awareness of how the

WORDS she used to describe herself were so powerful, she didn't care. She just wanted to be Right! Be careful. Don't be like my client and describe yourself with words (unconsciously) just because you and others have used them for a long time.

Don't allow others to create labels for you. When someone says something about me or gives me a label (you are .....) , I have two choices: one, argue with the person and defend myself and show her or him that I'm not that. Or, without getting into an argument, silently repeat to myself: "That's just his or her opinion. That is not who I am", and immediately, I repeat what I know myself to Be in a type of affirmation. Usually the opposite to the label.

What I discovered through my years of experimenting with communication and words is that it is not worth your time and energy to argue with someone who has a certain picture of you. Continue to live your life and demonstrate the opposite, if you desire. One of my pet-peeves is when others give labels to people. To be transparent, I have to let you know it took me many years to stop labeling others. Now I am so conscious not only of when I'm about to do it, but also when others do it. If it is done to a child, I take charge and correct it in front of the child. If it is done to an adult, I believe the adult has the responsibility to respond as he or she wishes.

In a conversation with a highly enlightened friend of mine, he made me realize that the word 'pet-peeve' represented those things I had reactions towards. He made me see how even when we are responding to what we believe is a loving reason, it is still a reaction and a judgment from our part.

After this conversation, I went deeper into observing my Words. How are they congruent to who I am and what I believe? I discover then that writing the Words I live for, or I intent to live for, keep me aware and conscious of my purpose in life.

Do I act incongruently sometimes? Unfortunately yes. All I know is that the incongruencies are becoming less and less. What's most important is the direction we envision. And as I said at the beginning, when the direction gets switch, we have the sharpest tool (our words) to get back to our true north.

One way to measure our congruency is this formula:

My Words + My Actions = My Results

A Disclaimer is necessary at this point:

When we are speaking words that describe our Vision as if it is happening in the present moment, and the material manifestation is not seen with our 5 senses, rest assured that it's on its way. It's a matter of opening yourself to receive it. We can receive the essence of what we desire before receiving the material manifestation.

An example: One of my clients told me that she wanted a large beautiful home and for years she asked for.

Next question to her was: 'why do you want this type of home'? What is the essence of what you desire?'

I don't know, she said.

"What if you knew"? I asked her.

"I want space to entertain, to create a space for inviting people from all over the world, to have a space for large crowds in my place and bring together people to share ideas, ideals, visions, and dreams".

"And what's stopping you from doing that right now?"

"Good question," she responded.

Two months later she called me to let me know that she was creating Online Webinars where she was talking and sharing with people from all over the world. The essence of her desire was manifested, though, in a different physical form.

When she realized what had happened, she let go of her anxiety for the big house, and 3 months later, she was living in her dream home.

How does this happen? It's all about awareness. It's all about paying attention. It's all about making our Words work for us.

Here Are Some Of the Words (Rules) I Live By or Intend (Consciously) to Live By:

I'm sharing this for the purpose of making myself accountable to the world. (*I will encourage you to choose a friend, coach, partner to make yourself accountable as well. Not that they will determine your outcomes, but that you will have a bar to measure your progress.*)

Everything happens for a reason.

There are no mistakes only opportunities to expand.

There are no failures only learning opportunities.

There are no obstacles only challenges.

Everything is possible with determination, persistence and courage.

Our Vision comes with its Provision.

I will *always* end my sentences in the positive regardless of what precedes them, i.e., It might be challenging AND I will still look into it.

Observe that the above statements leave you with a feeling of expansion not contraction. There is scientific proof that the brain opens up when we use the word AND as opposed to BUT, as well as when we end up our sentences in the **positive** (Can, possible, done, yes) as oppose to the negative (impossible, can't, no, difficult, etc.) **- Do not get hung up on the use of the words 'positive or negative' in the previous sentence. It was done for the purpose of demonstrating the point.**

The Veil is Lifted

As we take our masks off and let our true nature shine, our world transforms. Lifting the veil can be painful as we need to let go of the old to become ready for the new. Some things have to die, and in some cases, many things have to die. As we are ready to lift the veil so as to see with our inner eye instead of our outer eyes, many forces will try to stop us. Remember, we are at the beginning of our journey to freedom, our true wealth. Do not be surprised if you bump into some mountains. It is your *words* and the power you give to them, that it will help you overcome those mountains. Be prepared to sharpen your tool.

In my experience, the most challenging language to learn is the "inner language", that is, **the language you use to talk to yourselves.**

When do we learn about the "inner language"? Did you take classes when you were in school? How are we supposed to learn this language when it is rarely taught by our parents, or taught in formal classes during our early childhood?

To move from blaming others, circumstances, or our outer world, to taking full responsibility for our decisions, results, and life, it is essential that we first learn to communicate with our inner self. How about being compassionate with ourselves? Sometimes we are nicer to others, than we are to ourselves.

I met an amazing 75 year old lady, who is an author, writing a book on the Language of the Heart. To her, living in our power meant that we must first love ourselves before we can love someone else. That means that we choose to talk to ourselves with the same compassion and forgiveness that we give to others. It means that we choose to face our fears by changing our perspective with ease, tenderness, and patience. To her, loving ourselves was, and is, speaking the Language of the Heart.

How can we speak words of life if not by expressing them from the heart? How about embracing our challenges as well as our strengths? Loving our gifts as well as our shortcomings. Seeing the good in ourselves as well as the good in others.

What does it entail to get to this place of Inner Power? I questioned this for years. I knew I had to learn how to do this. I was determined to learn how so I could share my experiences with the world.

The Inner Language Rules - ILR

As it is required in any language, in order to speak a language correctly there are rules to follow, and they vary accordingly. For example, in English, adjectives do not have a gender differentiation, whereas in Spanish, if the noun is feminine or masculine, the adjective uses the feminine or masculine ending respectively. Rules are important to follow so as to convey messages correctly.

The same goes with the Inner Language, and when we learn the rules, we start to see things from a completely different perspective. I remember exactly when I learned the Inner Language Rules – I had a paradigm shift.

First of all, in psychology there is a talk about the inner language being the language of Understanding Emotions. In this respect, it refers to connecting with the inner language of others and being able to recognize whether they are visual, auditory, or kinesthetic, and as such responding to their needs based on their preference. That's one concept.

For the purpose of this topic, I am referring to Inner Language somewhat different. I'm talking about the Inner language as the language we use when we talk to ourselves. More specifically, how could we talk to ourselves authentically so we can find our true potential and live our purpose?

When you picture yourself as a diamond mine, what does it take to get to the actual rock, and what does it take to get it to shine as beautiful as the most expensive diamond? In other words, how could you go deep and discover who you truly are? How could you lift your veil and see from a different perspective?

Your "Inner Language Rules"

Steps you will go through as you speak to your inner self – Do not miss any of the steps until you get to #9.

1. "I don't know what's happening" - unawareness

2. Rejection to the first ideas that come to mind

3. Feel confused about the inconsistencies you find

4. Explore feelings of fear, doubt, unworthiness

5. Open-up to exploring— Surrender

6. Accept with compassion what you dislike

7. Understand that what is happening is happening for a reason

8. Explore possibilities that come to your awareness

9. Open up to the vast possibilities—Realize your human potential

'Getting Out of Your Way' - Exercise

When we 'Get Out of Our own Way', which means, we know who we are because we've taken the time to explore our fears, doubts, strengths and weaknesses; the road to our purpose is clear and wide. I heard people talking about 'Getting out of our own way', but I didn't know what it meant. I wanted to learn how to get to my purpose so I discovered the process I'm sharing with you here.

The way to conduct this exercise is with questions; open-ended questions that will ask for deeper answers within yourself. What is the situation?

When / Why do I feel certain way? (i.e. scared, hurt, anxious, worried, etc.)

Where do I hurt the most?

What if I look at 'this' another way (different perspective)?

Who is the only person responsible for this?

How do I bring myself to a place of gratitude?

What words would describe my 'new being' at this moment? For more examples of open-ended questions go to www.thesharpesttooltowealth.

How Did I Miss This One?

There is always a right time for everything that takes place in our lives. We cannot rush our transformation. Can we speed up a seed so that it sprouts faster? Equally timely is our realization of our choices and the power we have to manage them (with our Words). It is in the moment of our awakening that we question our past and look at our future, but with different eyes. We look at the past, not to spend time dwelling on our mistakes and failures, but finding out how to heal the hurts that have stopped us from flowering; and to the future, to bring our dreams, vision and purpose closer to our heart so that we can act intentionally and on purpose daily.

THE SHIFT

What do we experience when all of the sudden we are headed in a brand new direction? Have you ever experienced taking a road you have never taken? Do you remember this feeling? There is newness, there is surprise, there is the unknown—and there is also joy, wonder and expectancy. These are the feelings that come with the Shift, the turn, the new direction. Let me assure you that there will also be moments of fear, however, these moments become an opportunity to look within and find out the root of the experience. There is no more walking in the dark, instead everything becomes a possibility for growth, expansion, transformation.

In my case, it wasn't that one day I got up and everything was different, or that I was walking through the woods, and all of the sudden I began experiencing eternity. No. It was a gradual awareness and discovery of the consciousness that is based in abundance, oneness, connectivity, unconditional love, reverence for the goodness of others, and acceptance of the 'what is'. More specifically, I moved from wanting to change the world, to looking within myself to make changes I wanted to see in the world. It was moving from wanting to tell others, to only telling others if they asked. It was moving from sticking to my decisions even when others did not agree with them. It was being aware that as I value myself, I would not waste my energy with causes or ideas that don't resonate with my vision and purpose. Furthermore, it was understanding that the more I value myself, the more others value my work. And finally, it was reaching the knowing that nothing, absolutely nothing happens that I didn't attract into my life.

Having made this Shift, I was freed from wasting my energy arguing, convincing others, giving unsolicited advice, making others wrong, preaching to others (literally), in other words, consuming energy that I could be using in living my purpose.

This is not about being selfish, nor do I promote selfish behavior. Since this book is about the power of words, let us look at what the word 'Selfish' means in the original sense of the word: obsessive regard for the well-being of oneself without regard for the needs of others.

If 'being kind to ourselves' depicts being self-ish, then being self-ish is essential to our well-being. We cannot give others what we don't have. Can we give kindness when we don't even give it to ourselves? No. If you are someone who always put others first, regardless of whether you're hurting or not, I encourage you to evaluate your actions. We need to 'guard' our energy if we want to live from our true potential.

When I talk to others who have made the Shift, one of the first changes I notice is their ability to shift their perceptions with discernment. One action one time might not be the best action the second time. Be willing to adjust and discern your situation and your responses according to the present situation. The rules for living from a new consciousness are not written in stone—We actually began operating from intuition, from that inner voice, from that inner sense that guides us to right action, and not necessarily the easiest action.

The Tool = Freedom = Wealth

A tool is something used in the performance of an operation. Most of us need tools to assist us in accomplishing our daily tasks; so it is in our process of transformation, especially when we are heading towards freedom, and therefore wealth.

It is said that if we only have a hammer, everything we see will look like a nail; we will look for those things to hammer. However, as we get more tools, we have more choices. I always talk about my brother in law who has a knife for everything; a knife to cut bread, to cut meat, fish, a knife for steak and you get the idea. I'm sure many of you have these different knives. What calls my attention is that if I were to cut a tomato with the bread knife it was a no no. But in my Latin-American mentality, what's wrong with doing this? A knife is a knife is a knife. Not for my brother in law.

Why do I bring this example? It is the same in life. What is right for some, it might be wrong for others. I've learned to equip myself with as many tools as possible. The more the merrier. Why so? I can have access to the most appropriate one when required. I will always resort to the "Power of Words" as my first resource. Using the Words as my basis, I will combine any other one, either EFT (Emotional Freedom Technique), or NLP (Neuro-Linguist Programming), Muscle Testing, or Meditation and so on. I advocate that the larger our library of resources is, the more choices we have available to face events in our lives.

What I Thank Expands

It is not a mystery that what we are grateful for expands. It is actually scientifically proven that the energy of gratitude and appreciation works as a magnet, so in that respect, the more thankful and grateful we are towards something, someone, event, the more we attract such elements into our lives. If transformation is what we are headed for, as we thank the essence of what we are looking for, (i.e. love, peace, joy, prosperity, all elements of Wealth), it will undoubtedly manifest in our lives under the law that says, 'what we thank expands'. Do you see how our Words play a significant role into this effect? It is with our words that we express the gratitude felt deep in our hearts, therefore it is our attitude of gratitude expressed through our *words,* that which produces the results.

Put yourself through a rigorous discipline of thanking and being grateful about everything in your life, every aspect of your daily routine, and every circumstance that shows up. It is in this organized type of decision that you will find the value of disciplined focus on adding value to what you're receiving in your life; and furthermore, to expand into what's on its way by the law of attraction.

When we take this law seriously, we begin to experience its manifesting results. I remember when I began thanking and being grateful for the opportunity of being an agent of change and what I felt when I first heard clients calling me by these words. There is a feeling of oneness with the Whole when we get to experience the manifestation of what we've already thanked.

That everything we are grateful for is already in existence, it's something I continue to build on and experience as I become more and more attentive to what I ask for. Are you asking for what you want or are you asking for what you don't want? You might not be cognizant of what's happening with your results if you are not consciously aware of the power of your words. I encourage you, once again, to look at your life and those things you have manifested, and be honest with yourself, knowing that what is surrounding you at this particular time, it's exactly what you have asked for, not in your head, but in your heart. There is a big difference and it is all about the language we use.

I tended, for most of my life, not to ask for help. It could've been my fear of rejection or my pride. I now understand that both are the same—Fear of rejection so that I didn't feel hurt, and pride so that I didn't have to show my fear of rejection

Write it, Write it, Write it – It Can Only Grow!

Words that are written have life. Have you ever gone back to your journal or written material and be amazed of what you've expressed with your words? The amazing thing is that when we write, we allow the magic of our spirit guide us and therefore we obtain clarity and focus. Many experts suggest that we write in the middle of confusion, fear, despair, joy, gratitude, or love. Why? Because as we write, our words become alive on paper. Our words can be read again and again. Our words can show us where we are at a certain point in our lives. Transformation often happens as we explore where we have been and where we are heading, and what a better way than by reading what we have expressed in writing during our journey. It is our written words what keep the records of our path to transformation and growth.

Just a Little Adjustment – Daily Routine

As a mechanic turns a little screw and gets a car running, so it is with our lives. It often only takes a little adjustment to create outstanding results. What can we adjust? Our attitudes, our thinking, our perceptions, our paradigms. When we consistently adjust those little intricacies in our lives, we end up with a colossal new monument. In our lives, as with our cars, it is the little things that sometimes cause a blockage to a higher performance. When we want to get into higher gear, we need a mechanic. Preferably one who uses a tool that is at our disposition 24/7. That mechanic is us at a conscious state, or speaking from a spiritual perspective, our higher self, our God.

New Interpretations – New Results

*I gave a speech at a Toastmasters' competition where I talked about the healing power of changing the 'interpretation we give to words'. The speech was about a word (in Spanish) I heard during my childhood -- The word itself is not as important as the meaning **I attached** to it -- When I looked back at some of my decisions and incongruencies, many had to do with the destructive meaning and interpretation I had given to this word. Then, during an exercise on emotional healing, I went deep into different aspects of my life and found out that such word (and interpretation) was ingrained somewhere in my subconscious. During the exercise, I brought it up into my awareness, looked at it, changed the interpretation and meaning of it, and ended up freeing myself from a destructive attachment I had (myself) created.*

Your Word Interpretations and the Shift to Freedom / Wealth - Exercise:

- Do you have a word or label your parents, teachers or anyone in authority have said or given to you?

- Is it a diminishing label from your perspective?

- What did you observed, saw, felt that made you create that interpretation?

SHIFT - Look at it from a different perspective and consciously add a new interpretation to it.

- What you observed, saw, felt, at that time, could it have been your own interpretation? When your parents were upset, was it always with you or could it have been that they were under stress? When they looked or spoke certain way, was it because they didn't understand or knew a better way. Were they perhaps frustrated with themselves and took it upon you? etc.

- *Now, attach an interpretation that serves you.* For example: when my mother said 'X' she meant 'X'—She repeated a word that was said to her during childhood (unconsciously). *The new interpretation must always be something that serves you and builds you, removing pain and hurt.*

It takes creativity to change your interpretations and it is worth it. The change happens at a cellular level, and it is freeing. This is called, 'Taking your Power Back'. When we continue to feel pain because of someone's actions, we have given our power to them. We need to remember that it is always 'about us not the other'. The people we encounter in our lives are here for us to learn something. It is us the ones who need to make whatever change is necessary. We cannot wait for others to change. The power is in our own words—New Interpretations, New Results.

This exercise on 'changing our interpretations' can be used in all our interactions with coworkers, business partners, loved ones, etc.

Value of Words

To value is to appreciate. What if we consciously appreciate every word we utter? What would that mean to our language? How careful would we be with our communication? Is this what valuing our words really mean? If we were to give the same importance and care to our words as we give to the other things in our lives, our results will show accordingly. Have you ever heard someone constantly saying: if only I could. Has this person ever achieved anything significant in life? Or have you, on the other hand, heard someone saying: I know it is difficult, AND I will do it, anyways. What is the difference between these two statements? Can you see the power and intention conveyed in them? By appreciating the power of each word that comes out of our mouth, our awareness enhances and we develop an acute watchfulness towards our speech. Transformation doesn't happen by osmosis. It happens with our conscious use of our *words* and the sharpening of the process that takes to build the *world* that we envision.

Words have the power to limit our thoughts – similarly, and to a more enlightening end, our words act as the tool to build our vision and manifest our purpose and desires.

Transforming – Who? Myself?

Does the word 'transformation' scare you? Our bodies transform every seven days. We just don't get to see it, but biologically speaking, our body gets a new liver, new skin, new hair periodically. So why fear transformation? Is it a fear of losing who we are? Only when we get to know exactly who we really are do we look forward to transformation. In embracing transformation we become who we really are. It is an oxymoron, and one with which is better to live than to ignore.

Chapter Four
Now I Say It, Now I See It!

A Brand New World

Do you remember when you first landed at a place you've never been to before? Take a minute and bring back those memories— the ecstasy, the curiosity, the awe of seeing new things, of experiencing a different environment, the warmth or the cold, the smiles of the people, their looks— everything was new, everything was fresh. The same happens when we experience a brand new world within. We have the power to claim what we want to experience. We use our Sharpest Tool to Wealth, our Words, to create that magnificent experience we are looking for. The power is in our tongue. Why not use it? Can you imagine? Having the power to create any world you want to experience? Isn't that pure wealth? And it begins in your Inner World—When circumstances do not alter your 'Wealth-being'.

I Speak It Therefore I Create It

It sounds like magic, doesn't it? And it is like magic. It was Albert Einstein who said: "There are two ways to **live**: you can **live** as if nothing is a **miracle**; you can **live** as if everything is a **miracle**." - He didn't tell us how to do it, though. Now you know it – *'Speak it therefore you Create It'*—This is actually ancient wisdom. Jesus Christ said something like this, *I tell my people to speak what they want but they are speaking what they have.* He told us to claim our well being by speaking it into existence; believing it first and then seeing it manifested. We need to go beyond our five senses and believe in the energy and power of our Words. This is a constant reminder of a gift we have, that if not used, will be taken away.

Share Your Message

Each of us has a message in our heart. Each of us has a life that can be shared for the good of others. Each of us has learned strategies, life lessons, ways of going through challenges, ways of creating shifts, ways of living that can empower other human travelers. It is actually our responsibility to our Creator to pass on our life messages to others so that their lives are better. It is not a joke, it is a command. We were not created to pass by, but to make our Creator proud. Take this message seriously.

When I began taking this message to heart, I joined Toastmasters, an international organization dedicated to help its members learn and practice Public Speaking and Leadership. I had also joined Dale Carnegie Training where I learned how to communicate from the heart both personally and professionally. As I mentioned in my introduction, from the time I experienced Marc Victor Hanson, I made the decision to live a meaningful life and this meant that I was to share my journey with others. I became Purpose in Action.

Now I will be sharing a speech I've delivered for Toastmasters.

The Vision of our World is the Vision of our Words!

He was "Against" Slavery, read the article written about Abraham Lincon. Although this was an impacting cause - one he died for (Lincon was assassinated because of his advocacy against slavery in the 1800 hundreds), there was something about this sentence that brought me to a new realization.

After I finished reading the article in one of my classes today, I used the word "against" to make a point. I proceeded to share with the students what I was against, and began writing a list on the board. "I am against discrimination", I said. And as I was writing, I asked myself. What is the opposite of Slavery? Freedom, was the first word that came to mind. And I continue playing with the words.
All of the sudden while the students where working on one of the exercises, I remember something that Mother Teresa said. "Do not be against anything, but be For Something" So I proceeded to write. I am For Freedom and I am for Equality.

What took place at that moment was the recognition of the Power of our Words. What feelings did I have when I said 'Against' something as opposed to – 'For' something? Just in my body I could feel the reaction of my muscles. When I say 'I'm against something', my body contracts. I immediately go into a fighting position. My energy is about to face barriers, obstacles. To the contrary, when I say: 'I am For something', I see opportunities, I get ideas, I see possibilities. I feel optimistic. Even my body looks different. My face smiles when I say I'm for something. I'm for Freedom. When I say 'Against', my face gets hard, I make a fist, I hit my hands, Instead, as I say 'For', I open my hands and extend my arms.

What a realization! Mother Teresa was into something with the 'Power of Words'. I always remember what she had said, but this time, I'd actually experience it. I'm actually writing a book, many of you know, and this time, I actually got a Coach to help me finish it. In it, I will be talking about the fact that our Words create and that Words are the most important tool to create our Wealth. And I'm referring to Wealth as in well-being which encompasses all areas of our lives.

The experience this morning and how I felt is a practical example of the intrinsic value we give to words and the power or powerlessness they produce. How about the fact that very often we argue about something, only because we haven't clarified the meaning?

What if we are mindful of the words we use? Do they empower us or dis-empower us? Do they empower others or dis-empower others?

We have this powerful tool to create our destiny – Our Words – and as we become more conscious and watchful we build what we so much desire.

I'm aware and have talked about the power of our thoughts and how they create our lives. And how about the power of our Words? How is it that we manifest our thoughts? Is it not with our Words? Words are actually the manifestation of our thoughts. Out of our mouth, our heart speaks!

Listen to others and find out who they are, what they have, and where they're going. You can find out about people's dreams, fears, ambitions, challenges. I remember meeting a public speaker and leader one time who said: 'give me five minutes with someone, I will tell you about his or her destiny'.

True Wealth is about life balance in the four important areas of our life: mental, emotional, spiritual and physical($). Most of us know people who have a lot in one area but are struggling in another. Could we call these people Wealthy? To be truly wealthy we need to know how to use the resources we have available to us. We've been given an incredible resource, one I call 'The Sharpest Tool to Wealth' - Our words. As with any treasure, we need to treasure our Words; they are our destiny!

The vision of our world is the Vision of our Words.

Life or Death Is In the Power of the Word

To speak life or to speak death only requires that we use different words. Words cut like a knife or can bring light like a lamp. Understanding that we have such power in something we get to create, our words make us responsible for what we build or destroy. Do we build dreams, or destroy them with our words? Do we build people or destroy them with our words? Do we build hope, or despair with our words? Do we create love, or fear with our words? We have this power. Use it properly.

If I Can Name It, I Can Have It

Dale Carnegie, a well-known author in the field of communications, was adamant to the fact that if we don't use a person's name, that person doesn't really exist. It goes with everything else. If we don't name what we desire, how can we have it, or manifest it, or experience it, or even recognize it when is in front of us? The beauty of all of this awareness is the knowing that in the universe everything already exists. It is our job to name it so we can manifest it. This might sound a little esoteric for some, but the reality is that when we know that everything we are searching for is searching us, our job is to name it, claim it, recognize it, and be thankful for.

One more thing. Don't describe your life. Design it! When you are constantly describing your life, that's where you will be. There is no sense of movement. There is no sense of going anywhere. You become stuck.

How do you begin to move forward? Speaking your vision with your own words. Begin writing and speaking the lifestyle that you envision. See yourself not as you (think) you are at this moment but as you know in your heart you could be; that potentiality that can create whatever you imagine. As a Coach, I am always holding my clients at a higher place than they can see themselves, until they believe it is possible for themselves. It is often our own limitations what stop us from breaking through; however, when we learn how to use the dialogues of our life in certain way, we can create our own breakthroughs. Do you want to be free from fear? Say it. 'I Am Free from Fear'. Do you want to be a business person travelling all over the world? Claim it as if you were already that – 'I am travelling all over the world'. Would you like to have a harmonious relationship at work and at home?

Speak it into existence. Write down and read it morning and evening. Have a picture of your desire and hold it in your mind with your words; speak it with others and to others so it cements in your mind. This is how you build the new you. This is how you uncover the real you.

> Stop Describing yourself, instead, Design yourself

Quality of Life Determined By Quality of Questions

Picture this – someone asks you, *"What are your possibilities?"* Right after, *"What are your problems?"* Feel the essence of each of these questions. Which one is expansive, which one is contriving? Did you know that Human Resources experts understand this power of questioning very well and, therefore, during a job interview for example, orchestrate their questions carefully according to what they are looking for in a person?

As well, the questions we ask ourselves could be even more powerful than the questions others ask us. Be fearless when questioning yourself and conscious of what you are looking for. Which combination of Words are you using when you question yourself? Or, do you even question yourself? Are your questions ones that bring clarity or confusion? Are they creating fear or love? Are they bringing you to life or death? You can decide what to ask depending on what you want to see manifested in your own life.

It is worthwhile noting that if you are searching for answers it is better to use 'How' questions as opposed to 'Why' questions. 'How' questions put us in a creative mode. We receive answers and we are then responsible for taking action once the way is shown. 'Why' answers tell us that something was done certain way or could be done differently but doesn't show us the way.

Examples: How could I create more joy in my life? How could I bring more harmony into my life? How could I understand 'x' better? How could I create new streams of income? Etc. Remember, the sharpest tool to wealth is your words - use it to your own benefit, especially when you are questioning yourself. Do not turn your words into your enemy. It's all about being conscious to this awareness. Experiment with different questions and see the difference. The deeper your awareness, the easier to 'get out of your own way' and get to your true potential.

Me? An Exceptional Conversationalist?

Have you ever thought of yourself as a conversationalist or someone who could hold a conversation with a stranger? All you have to do is to learn how to ask questions. This little secret was revealed by Anthony Robbins, a world re-known motivational speaker and self-help author. How does this work? You can create a better dialogue and connection when you become *interested in people*, rather than when your aim is for *you to become interesting to others*. Rarely do others want to hear all about you unless they have a specific interest and have asked you to share. If you are the one to become the exceptional conversationalist, begin by focusing on others' interests and finding out what makes them tick. How? - By using the *"Conscious Questioning Process"*™. Let's remember: our greatest resource is people. By becoming an exceptional conversationalist we become open to Wealth.

Session II: Talking to Others

Chapter Five
If It Wasn't For You

When Perceptions Transform

Our perception is a system of knowledge and beliefs based on our own experience. It is the internal map we use to create actions and behaviors. It is our personal reality. Why is that two people can look at the same thing, and get a different response? Interestingly enough, it is because of their different perceptions. Many arguments are caused because we don't take the time to understand the perceptions of others. This is detrimental to our relationships, this is detrimental to our Wealth; and this is detrimental to our Being. As we transform our perceptions, we create what is called a 'paradigm shift'. In other words, we change the patterns in which we respond to what we perceive - this is Wealth, this is Freedom.

The meaning we assign to words depends on our experiences; this is our challenge when we talk with others who have *completely* different experiences than ours. Our Metaphors have the power to create our realities. What's the first thing that comes to mind when you use each of the different metaphors? (below). Experiment with the feeling that each phrase creates in you. Go ahead.

Life is an Adventure
Life is a Miracle
Life is Hard
Life is like a River
Life is a Blessing; etc.

Any particular realization after experimenting with the metaphor exercise? I remember when I changed my perception of the word 'selfish' to 'self-care'. My actions automatically took a different direction. Changing the perception of one word changed my results. I went from being afraid of being 'selfish' to taking actions that represented 'self-care', and feeling good about myself.

The World of New Paradigms

Are you ready for a change? *"Change your words change your world"*™ - That's where we start.

Do you want a New World? You have the power to create it. What do you see with your five senses? Go beyond them and begin building with your mind's eye. Use the words that describe the experience you want to have. Use the words that help you create a special feeling; a feeling of high vibration where everything that belongs to you is attracted. Use the words that bring you, in your mind, to that World you know exists already. Is a world of harmony and wealth you're looking for? Create it with your words - first in your mind, and then in your physical life as it manifests. It is a law. It won't fail you. Live your new paradigm, the new way of looking at things, the new way of responding to what you perceive. It is possible and it is your Wealth.

I remember when I realized that I had to become bolder in order to live my purpose. From my desire to please others, or fear of being rejected, I would easily bend to the wants of others. This was done unconsciously, of course. As I became 'Present' and started paying attention and honoring my Purpose, I began to value and respect my wishes and the direction my life was taking.

You and I Are One

The I in you is the I in me. How do I know this? Try it for yourself. Think of one person. Think of everything you like about that person and everything you dislike about them. Go deeper. Really look close at what you're seeing, and how you are feeling. Those things you like about the other, deep in your heart, you love in yourself. Similarly, those things you don't like about the other, you don't like about yourself. Do you know why, when you go for a job interview, the interviewer asks you what you liked about your previous boss?

The interviewers know that the exact words you use to describe your boss are the exact same things that describe you. If there are personality traits you dislike, that is exactly what you would dislike not only of your new boss, but of yourself. The question serves two purposes, one, to get to know you better, two, to understand who you would work best with.

It's not a secret that what we see in others is only a reflection of who we are (in terms of personality). I'll make the distinction later on in the book between personality and who we really are (our true nature). What's essential to understand is that we are not separate by any means. The more we want to see our separateness the more obvious our oneness becomes.

The word 'Oneness' carries such power that when we say it, attracts the energy of 'togetherness' almost by osmosis.

Your Words Reflect My Other Self

The Other Self is that part of us which we don't see clearly. It's that part of ourselves, that blind area of which we are unaware. Using the Johari Window—a graphic model of awareness and cognitive psychological tool by Joseph Luft and Harry Ingham, used to help people better understand their interpersonal communication and relationships, the Other Self is that part of ourselves, that blind area, of which we are unaware. This is the reason we have to be grateful for having people in our lives who reflect back to us that part that is hidden from our awareness. Our so called 'enemies' are really gifts, only and when we learn to appreciate them for showing up in our lives for a specific purpose. What if we make use of this awareness and welcome all kinds of people into our lives with an attitude of gratefulness? Would the world be different? What stops us from doing that? That is worth exploring.

My Words Only Express Who I Am

"Don't worry—what I say to you is not who you are, but who I am", taking this axiom to heart is the path to true freedom from the opinions of others, which ultimately leads you to Wealth. Breaking free from taking things personally creates space for your mind and spirit to create anything from your heart, where true greatness resides.

In past pages, the spoken word was considered a tool to create our wealth through the dialogues we have with ourselves. In this Session II: **Talking to Others**, our wealth is created by using our words consciously, but more importantly, becoming aware of how we talk to each other and receive messages from others. We need to remember that communication is a two-way street. It never happens in isolation. Even in our Session I: **Talking to Ourselves**, there is the I and the Observer. Even when it's just yourself, there is still a two-way communication. In fact, *all conversations are with me first and then with others*. In other words, I go through all my values, beliefs, fears, emotions, before I communicate with others. This happens in a millisecond timeframe. As we learn to live in the Present Moment, this process gets shorter and shorter, and we speak from that place that is Here and Now with no past nor future.

This is what living in the Present Moment means—we are hundred percent who we truly are in our essence: joy, peace, love, abundance, freedom. Created beliefs disappear, or we have the power to change them as we wish; emotions from the past don't come up, or if they do, we observe them, they don't control us; value judgments are non-existent; there is only 'Presence'.

Wealth Spreads in Words

How amazing is that Wealth can be spread in Words. What is the implication when we believe this? We can have Wealth at our disposition for us and for others. Let me explain. Have you seen the face of a child when parents praise him or her for a job well done? Consider this an act of spreading Wealth with Words: 'well-being' translates into wealth; in fact, 'well being' is wealth. We have at our disposal a tool to spread Wealth. The more we use it, the better and more effective will become. If our words are the Sharpest Tool to Wealth, all we have to do is use it with others. This practice will help us sharpen it even further, which in turn will translate into more wealth. The law says: "That which we give, returns to us multiplied".

You Helped Me Grow – You Are My Teacher

The best and most effective way to grow is in a relationship. How else will we be able to find out about those areas that require transformation, attention, awareness? In isolation we could only become aware of what we can see for ourselves. It was Einstein who said: "We cannot alter a condition with the same mindset that created it in the first place." This goes to say that, as we change our perspective, the vision of our intricacies is more complete. Seeing our own weaknesses requires careful introspection. It is, nonetheless, not so difficult for someone else to be ready to point out our rough spots to us, even when we're not asking; as we mentioned before, just look at what you don't accept in others. Teachers emerge from what we sometimes call our 'enemies'. The people that can irritate us have a valuable message for us. Let's not avoid them because we will be wasting a valuable gift – a piece of Wealth.

I have a friend who showed me how being in a relationship is the most effective spiritual path anyone can choose. Barbara would point out to me how the people who 'push our buttons' (irritate us) the most are those closest to us. How so? They are the

74

ones who we attracted into our lives for a specific purpose—To allow us to grow and expand. To show us our darkest places. To allow us to see ourselves in the mirror. Recently I heard a speaker say, "Opposites attract, but in marriage, opposites attack." This was said as a joke, but really, doesn't that seem to be true? It feels like an attack when the other uses certain type of communication which is really showing us what we dislike about ourselves.

Most recently, I was carefully listening to the words my "opposite" was using in a particular conversation, and all of the sudden I realized that I was despising his words. Why? I perceived that his intention was to despise me because he, somehow, was hurt. As soon as I came to this realization, I concentrated on helping him heal his hurt and stopped focusing on what he was saying, and concentrated on his feelings. This was a powerful remedy. The tool I used was, you guessed it—Words to build him. Words that soothed him. Words that showed my love and respect for him. The result? A more compassionate relationship from both sides.

Words That Get Us Closer

"Words cut like a knife and also can heal like the sun" —EM

There are words that are like honey, and not because they build our ego or make us feel good, but because they cut right through our spirit and build up our strength, love, and acceptance. It might be a sentence such as "tell me more", "I believe in you", "you can do it". Our hearts dance the dance of love but we need to sing the music to ourselves and to others. What music are you playing? What lyrics are you singing? Do they get you close to others or do they push you away?

But do all of us want to hear the same Words? Do Words motivate us all the same? As a Behavioral Specialist, certified in a number of behavioral systems, I understand that Words work differently for different personalities. This is a complex realm and one that it's been highly applied in the workplace for the purpose of team development and personal and professional development in general.

From the premise that each of us is different, and that there are certain elements of our personality that are triggered differently from each other, I'd like to touch on this subject.

There are some who are motivated by action and therefore will be motivated through action words.

There are those who are motivated by involvement, excitement, and therefore will be motivated by words of involvement, excitement, enthusiasm.

There are those who are motivated by accuracy, perfection, and logic and therefore will be motivated by words that depict such values.

And there are those who are motivated by helping, serving, and supporting others, and therefore get inspired and motivated by words that relate to feelings, service, and collaboration.

So you see? When I talk fast, with words of pure excitement and action to someone who is centered on feelings, what happens? The person could get a bit discouraged. If I talk about feeling words to someone who is in need for action and results, what happens? Frustration. And what happens when I talk to someone who needs clarity and precision and I'm talking about excitement or feelings, what happens? Irritation. And for the one that desires excitement, if I come to this person with precision, logic or accuracy, what then? Confusion.

So you see.   People are complex, and as such we need to understand, if we desire to connect with others, a bit more about the intricacies of our human differences.

Go to www.thesharpesttooltowealth.com to find more details about these differences and how to connect using specific **WORDS**.

Here Is the Other Side—But What About Feelings?

Even though behavioral experts believe that we are all different and act differently according to our predominant personality, there are others who attest that we are mainly "Human Feelings", regardless. Many have said we are Human Beings, others have said, we are Spiritual Beings and so on. This question is to prompt you to expand your perspective as to how you see yourself and others.

Because of our complexity, the most important awareness we can reach as we read this book, is that we can change our perspective as we learn and appreciate new things, concepts, ideas, and from a new point of view. This reminds me of the process of evolving which resembles the process of peeling an onion. As we hear something new, we look at it, we either accept it or reject it, and we either apply it or not, we get rid of old ideas to make room for new ones; we change the old for the new.

It is, nonetheless, my recommendation that you take action when new ideas are presented and accept them because it is in the action (sometimes risky actions) that we discover who we truly are. It is not in the world of knowing that we expand. We stay there, and in fact we regress. It is in the venturing into the world of newness that we discover our Unlimitedness.

Getting right into the topic—There is a difference between 'I feel' and 'I think I feel'. 'I think I feel', is still a head thought not exactly a feeling—you will find that these distinctions are often made by those who are primarily motivated by Feelings.

Being with people involves being with our feelings and their feelings, together, on some kind of alternating, on-going level. My friend Peter said one time, 'People bring us problems'. I'm not sure if I completely agree with this; you know by now that I respect the energy words convey, but what he meant was that human beings are complex creatures and as such bring complexities into our lives.

An important part of relating to people is letting them know we are aware of their feelings – and by doing this in such way that they don't wish they had kept their feelings hidden. Humans are *feeling* beings (deep down, all of us are). Experiencing, expressing, and acting on feelings is an important part of living humanly. Many of us have been taught to hide, control, or change our feelings—rather than experience, express, and act on them. I'd like to make a distinction between 'act' and 'react'. Sometimes we try to be courteous, diplomatic, and helpful, instead of relating to each other as people with feelings. In my case, I was completely unaware of the world of feelings until I consciously began learning about the language of Feelings. Learning this language became challenging to me in that it took, exploring within, going deeper and getting to know and reveal myself—Something I didn't know how to do.

We function more appropriately when we are aware of feelings and let the other person know it. We benefit from showing acceptance of our own and other people's feelings. For years, as I mentioned, I had difficulties with the Language of Feelings. I didn't know how to use it. I actually had to consciously learn this language. For the most part, my responses would "cut off" the feelings of others, and the results were detrimental to my relationships. The sad part of all of this is that I didn't know I was acting this way until it was pointed out to me. This happened when I was interacting unconscious of the other persons' triggers and motivations.

When we show acceptance of other's feelings, we become closer in our relationship with them. When we don't show acceptance, we run into the danger of impoverishing our lives and the lives of others.

So What Does It Mean By Showing Acceptance? Acceptance of What?

Acceptance is realizing that others had different feelings than mine and that they had the right to feel "this" way. I didn't have to argue with their feelings nor did I need to make them feel differently or cure them of their feelings. Once I understood this, a lot of weigh was lifted from my shoulders. Why did I take on the responsibility of others' feelings? Why was I uncomfortable when I saw someone sad? Why did I want to fix the pain of others? Who told me I needed to be responsible for others' way of being? I don't know when I got these instructions but it took me a while to let this one go. It means I wanted to control others, under the disguise of being caring and thoughtful. Of course, this was Greek to me because I didn't understand any of what I'm just explaining to you. I thought I was being a 'good person', and that is what I strived to be. Unknowingly what I was being was a controlling woman.

Remember I mentioned that this book will lead you to Freedom? You can see how I became freer as I became conscious of all the behaviors that put me in a 'prison-like' life (What a metaphor. I just realized what it was like for me before I woke-up from a sleep-like life).

When we care we pay attention. Following are responses that 'cut off feelings' and make others feel we are not loving or compassionate:

Giving advice cuts off feelings. Giving reassurance shows no awareness of feelings.

Agreeing vigorously. The person may feel we are not interested in them as a person.

Feeling obligated to **act** on their **feelings**. We assume we have to do something: solve their problem, perform a task, etc.

I used these responses often and it took me a while to understand the consequences of doing this. It was about unawareness more than anything else. It was about wanting to stop others from hurting, but using my Own Way. What a misconception. Thinking that my way was their way. This belief and behavior cost me a lot of relationships and I suffered constant misunderstandings.

On the other hand, I got a hold of Dr. Marshall B. Rosenberg's Nonviolent Communication programs and the Spiritual Basis of his teachings—he states that our most basic spiritual need is to contribute to the well being of others and ourselves. (From my perspective, this is one way of accessing the Wealth Switch). While experiencing Dr. Rosenberg's teachings, I got a new level of awareness. Remember, I didn't know how to talk about feelings. I wasn't familiar with the Language of Feelings. Another language to learn. Does this seem like a lot of work? When we have a purpose and a vision, it is not work, instead it is a journey. I used to call it an 'adventure', and using this word gave me certain mindset and strength to go on. You see, I use my words to create my mental attitudes, and it works for me.

Dr. Rosenberg says: *acknowledge* the feelings of others during your interactions in order to create a connection. "I can see you are hurt", "I feel you are disappointed", "I can see you are angry". Acknowledge the feeling (first) before going any further with your conversations. I had a challenge with this process for a while, and as I tested it, I found out I was able to connect at a deeper level. I began using it, although it was risky for me to even try it. I received responses such as, "I'm not hurt. I'm not disappointed". This gave me the chance to say, "I misjudged my perception, sorry." After this, we continued connecting. How does this work? You'll have to experience it. Some people may respond positively, some might respond negatively. That's Ok.

Our actions and responses are situational, thus our need to "be fully present". How we respond in one situation doesn't have to be the same as in another situation. Any strategy without "being present", meaning completely connected, won't work. In my research regarding the aspect of "Feelings", I came across with some valuable material. I studied it and began to apply it in my daily life. Big changes began to take place—We often cannot tell where the best solution will come until we try it.

Here are some aspects of Feelings I discovered:
We suppress and release feelings for a number of reasons:

- Too much dependency on others for affection, for solution of problems, and for satisfaction of needs.

- Excessive fears of rejection; extreme fears of criticism; demands of a conscience, a 'world of shoulds'; a self ideal acceptance only (I can accept myself only as kind, generous, strong, so I suppress all other feelings producing guilt, producing threats to my self concept).

When we suppress our feelings in our interpersonal relationships we impoverish our lives and the lives of others; we relate to others impersonally and shallowly; we produce our own illnesses, and we could get out of control, thus, uncontrollable emotional outburst will occur.

How does all of this relate to our Words and the powerful tool they are in creating our Results?

Our words, NOT used with precision, create collision. A precise description of our feelings will make us look at them objectively and go to the root of the problem more easily than if we don't do it in a precise manner. Hiding our feelings causes us a lot of unconscious 'dis-ease'. In fact, it has been discovered that our diseases are caused by certain (negative) kind of feelings locked in our body. They get stored in our cells, unknowingly of the results they produce, until we find ourselves with the disease.

Our job is not to ignore the feelings. Our job is to recognize them, and consciously, take the time to transform our feelings into a state of well-being that serves us. Here is when the Words we speak become 'the tool' to access that place within, where harmony, joy, and unconditional love reside, regardless of our circumstances. Once that place is reached, our feelings are transformed and we begin to vibrate at a higher level where our Inner Wealth resides.

Steps to transforming your Feelings to get to a state of 'Wealth-Being'

1. Ask yourself the following questions:
   - How Am I feeling right now?
   - Why am I feeling this way? (*Why* question only conscious of how to use it)
   - What is my perception of the situation?
   - Am I willing to change my **perception** of this situation?
   - What is another way of looking at this situation?
   - How do I feel when I look at the situation from a different point of view?

2. As I have the CHOICE to look at my situation differently, and change my vibration and feelings by doing that, I **Choose** to exercise this power, and I use **Words** as my tool.

3. **We attract the energy we're vibrating at.** Some say, the lucky get luckier. I say, the wealthy (as in this book) get wealthier – that is, when we maintain certain state of mind, we will attract certain results. Exercise the Power of Choice. This power was given to us by our Creator.

Chapter Six
People Are Not Strange,
People Are Different™

Where Do You Come From?

This question conveys curiosity for some and isolation for others. Again, the meaning we give to words depends on our own experiences and perceptions. What if you come from a country or culture that has been ostracized? What if you come from a place where there has been violence? What if you don't feel proud of your country? But of course, we cannot allow circumstances to determine our self-worth and our perceptions. We have the power to turn things around with the *words* we utter and the meanings we give to them. This is only up to us, no one else. As author, William H. Johnsen said, *"If it is to be, it is up to me."*

In my last trip to Mexico, we were having lunch at a beautiful dining room with a glass window facing a large green tree that seemed to speak to us, its leaves waving softly and its flowers shining radiant through the sun. It was an amazing view. I was sitting in the middle and was the only foreigner (not from Mexico). As usual, I would ask, "So where are you from?" Most everyone answered assertively, telling me a bit about each city. I was happy to hear their stories, until I got to a lady who said, "I'm from X city but have been living here for many years." This answer sounded a bit defensive to me, so later on, I approached Maria (not her real name) and asked her again (when she was by herself). In a somewhat angry voice she said to me, "Many people make fun of me because I come from X city. I don't know what it is that people think we are," and she went on and on as to how she felt, because others made her feel inferior.

This of course was an opportunity for me to listen to her feelings first, and then explain how no one has the power to make us feel any way. I talked to her about the power we have with our words, and asked her if she wanted to conduct an experiment with me. She got excited and of course she agreed. Next morning as we got into the training session, I asked everyone where they came from. I had already coached Maria how to answer with precision and assertiveness in her voice, holding her own power in the words she spoke, and conveying certainty in what she was saying. The results were amazing. She got up, and with great confidence she spoke loudly and with certainty when her turn came up. Everyone clapped at the end since she spoke so beautifully and powerfully about the place she was born.

What a change, what a switch, what a paradigm shift. This experience confirms that where we come from does not determine who we are. For some, it might determine how they feel, however we have the Inner Power to change our Perceptions and the **Tool** is the **Words** we use. Tip : When others are reluctant to tell you where they come from it might be because they don't feel comfortable. A friend who has done a lot of cross-cultural work gave me a suggestion: instead of asking, "Where are you from? Ask, *"Are you from here?"* Asking this way makes it easier for others to answer as they choose.

You Are Not Alone

There are two basic human needs that make us all the same: our need to Love and our need to be Loved. No matter where you come from or where you have been, nothing, absolutely nothing can remove this need from your spirit. I've had the opportunity to ask this question, "what is your most prevalent need", to people from all walks of life and cultures, and the answers have been consistent: "to love and be loved", have they replied. That means that there will always be someone like you who has the same needs. In fact, we are all connected, and as we explore further the essence of what we're made of, there is no room for doubt that the connection is even stronger than what some of us might want to admit.

We Are All In This Together

The world cannot revolve around us all the time. We need to revolve around the world. What does that mean? As our awareness becomes more acute, we realize that what happens to one happens to all. Imagine having an attitude of oneness. What difference does it make? How will our actions be different when we know that we are not here for ourselves but for the entire humanity? How would your role in society change when you begin seeing through these glasses? What would your thoughts be when you have the awareness that they affect others? We are on this (path) together. We are fellow travelers whether we like it or not.

How Does This Feel For You?

When our consciousness focuses its attention in a particular way, that in turn causes the energy to localize in a particular form (Energy Consciousness). Where are we focusing? Can we actually use our words to point us in the direction of oneness? Can we use our words to direct us towards Wealth? Remember, what we focus on, expands. What a better tool to use in focusing us towards what we desire than our sharpest one– our Words! Isn't this freedom revealing to the upmost? Isn't this Wealth to the maximum? We not only need to feel empowered but also enlightened with this awareness. When oneness is our focus, people become our greatest resource, and vice-versa, we become the greatest resource to others.

Is This 'Greek' to You?

Not understanding others can be frustrating. If there was only one language in this world, how awesome would that be? Not quite! It is not our language what creates distances, or hurt, or joy and togetherness. It is the *intention* with which we use our words. Even when words don't mean the same, the emotion can be transmitted some how. Years ago, a new language called Esperanto emerged with the hope that people around the world could communicate easily among each other. It was to unify communication. Why didn't Esperanto survive and expand? I'm still questioning this.

Let Me Build a Bridge

Why is it that you don't hear me? I've been asked this question in different occasions. When this happens to me, I'm called to be aware of the 'attitude' of my communication, much more than the process. When my attitude is not that of bridging or connecting, there is always a breakdown in my conversations. I made my intention, during any type of communication, to always create connection and rapport first and then get to business. We might ask these questions from time to time or someone might've said this to you. Communication is like a present—Unless we unpack it, we don't get to its essence. For communication to work as a bridge, it needs to be more than a process. Effective communication is an attitude and desire to connect with others. Watch out. Not everyone communicates (connects) the same way, not everyone delivers and receives messages the same way; not everyone hears the same. Wonder why there are so many new behavioral programs getting us to become aware and awakened to our differences.

It was only a couple months ago when I had a conversation with my son. For years he had been telling me that I did not listen to him. We were both fed up. He, because I didn't listen; I, because I didn't know how to talk to him. This situation drove us to have a "serious conversation". I then created some space to evaluate this situation. During this time, I realized that all the training I was delivering to corporations was not doing anything to my private life, with the closest members of my family. Can you imagine? Being a Communications Specialist and not being able to communicate with your own son? Just before our last conversation, I said to him, "*You need to teach me how I need to listen to you."* His response, *"This is the first time you've asked me this."* Light came over! A bridge was built. Now we're talking! I recognized that I didn't know how to communicate with him, nor did I care before, it seemed like, to him.

So what bridge are we talking about? Let our actions speak louder than our words. Our words need to be congruent with our actions otherwise, it is all a façade.

Want To Connect?

To show that we are friendly, or that we at least acknowledge the presence of someone, we exchange words. "I see you and I am friendly," is in effect what the speaker is conveying when saying, "How are you?"or "Hello," or "Nice day." But is this enough, or is this just a formality?

Connecting entails much more than just formalities, and the words we use, either give birth to that connection or create a barrier.

Here is a **Speech** given to a Toastmasters' audience:

Be an Amazing Conversationalist

First of all, how many of you believe that it is important to be able to 'Converse with Ease'?

Have you ever been with someone whom you felt, after you left the conversation, that he or she was an amazing conversationalist?

Think about it -- What did he or she do that made you feel this way?

Listened to you!

This is the most revealing secret of 'How to Become an amazing Conversationalist'. What a paradox—become an amazing conversationalist by becoming a good listener.

I used to believe that to be a great conversationalist, I had to be knowledgeable on many topics. Or that I had to be aware of the latest news and hot topics of the week, or the month, or the year.

And imagine, even more challenging, not having the English language as a new immigrant in Canada, I thought, How am I going to meet strangers? Of course, I was afraid of meeting new people, or having to be in a group where I didn't know much of what was going on.

*I knew I had to find a solution to this fear, so I began searching for Communications training where I could learn how to speak properly, until I realized that it wasn't about "Speaking but Listening" which made the big difference. **This realization freed me from my fear of meeting strangers at any level**—In one of my first jobs in Canada, I was exposed to meeting executives who came from different countries, so I needed to have a strategy, or as I call it now, a different Awareness and Perspective.*

*What was the **Solution?***

When meeting (new) people:

Be Present
Ask Questions
Listen

Because:

- *How do you feel when people pay attention to what you're saying?*

- *How do you feel when people are curious about what you're saying?*

- *What are people telling you about you when they listen?*

- *What do you experience when a person tells you - tell me more?*

Go back mentally and think of those people who seem to be great conversationalists. What did they do? Were they the ones speaking all the time or were they the ones listening?

Some of you might ask. So if everyone is asking questions, who will be doing the speaking?

*When we are **Present, Ask questions, and Listen** in order to connect, a natural balance is created between the people conversing. It sometimes happens that one person will say, "I've been speaking a lot about me, how about you?" Here is your time to share, and you can end up your conversation with a new question.*

One time someone asked me. What would you say to a "very important" person you meet for the first time?

Here is what I would ask him or her: "What did you do to get to where you are?" "What brought you success?" "What brought you here?" "What's the secret to your success?"

Most people like to talk about their journey, especially if they find it exciting. I've never found a person who gets upset because I'm interested **IN** him or her, have you? Remember. It is important to "be Present" to maintain the conversation because it takes "curiosity" and a "genuine interest in others".

Dale Carnegie, the author of "How to win friends and Influence People" said that it is better to be **Interested IN people** than be interesting TO people.

In communications we talk about 4 communication phases:

1. The Small Talk or chit-chat

2. Disclosing Facts

3. Sharing Opinions

4. Sharing Feelings

For each of these phases, it is important to "Be Present and Ask Genuine Questions". Even when I ask, "How are you doing?" I pay close attention. I've seen people replying to, "How are you doing?" with "Not so good," and the other saying, "That's great!"

It becomes even more important to "be Present and ask questions Consciously" when we get to the other 3 levels where we begin to establish *a deeper connection — a word of advice: use 'open-ended' questions to keep the communication flowing with ease (what, where, when, who, why & how).*

In my experience, it is not so much the process that's important, but the attitude we have during our conversations.

The attitude to become an Amazing Conversationalist requires "Being Present and Genuine Interested IN others.

It is said that people don't remember what we say, but HOW we made them Feel.

Next time you meet someone, get out of your way and focus on the other person. This is the Secret to becoming an Amazing Conversationalist.

When You Desire What I Desire

Are we in the same boat? Does it mean that I have to agree with you? Do we have to think the same and desire the same things? Not necessarily. Bottom line, what most of us desire is that our way of communicating is respected. That you will not be forced to speak like I do, and each of us respect and accept that we can have different communication approach.

It took me years to learn how to speak using 'I' as opposed to generalizing with the 'we', especially when it came to diminishing statements, for example: we are so careless, or we are so disorganized, we are so..., etc. I learned how to use 'I' to own my feelings, responses, and choice. However, I recently spoke with a friend who mentioned that she had taken the 'I and the Me' out of her emails to become less demanding and more inclusive in her writing. It's this contradictory? It appears so, but in reality it's not. It takes understanding of when to use each approach accordingly. When I'm working as part of a team, I use inclusive vocabulary, 'we and us'. When I'm expressing feelings, choices, responses, I take responsibility for those, therefore, I speak using 'I and me'. As I became aware of this difference, my interactions became more authentic and therefore wealthier.

How Can I Understand You?

In his re-known book *"Men are from Mars, Women are from Venus"*, the author John Gray asserts that the first step to understanding someone is accepting our differences. Cultures that are heavily homogeneous as opposed to multicultural tend to have a more difficult time accepting differences among individuals. The collective society tends to put people into a mold where being the same is rewarded more so than being different. The path to understanding others requires the understanding of 'ourselves' first. Thus, the winding road we need to travel in order to understand our fellow human beings.

To add to the complexity of cultures, how about the generational differences. We now have Generation Y also called Millennial (1977 – 2000), generation X (1965 – 1977), Baby boomers (1946 – 1964) and traditionalists, (Before 1946) each with its own idiosyncrasies. Each of these generations requires different communication style which entails different use of our Words. For instance, Gen Y and X are much more informal than past generations. Focused on collaboration, this generation requires high levels of dialogue, compared to Baby boomers where decisions tend to be more individualistic. This is only one example

of the complexities we face in our understanding of others. It is
therefore essential that we discover much more than likes and
dislikes when we are communicating with others since a large
portion of what we don't know about others plays such a defining
role in our interpersonal connections.

Chapter Seven
How About Being the Same?

Our Essence, Our World

What the world is made of, so are we. In fact, we are the world. There is nothing earth shuttering about this statement, sometimes, some us forget that we are not separate from the world we live in. We create our world. The essence of the world is us and is *in* us. How could we ever forget that beautiful song *"We are the World. We are the Children. We are the ones that make a brighter day so let's start giving…"*

One of my clients told me of a presentation she participated in. She had to prepare a speech in two different ways. One was in English and the other one was in another language (whether she new the other language or not, was not important). The objective was for her to say it, even saying, "la la lalala la la", if necessary. At the end of the exercise (the second speech), even when no one understood what she had said, the audience sensed her spirit and inner energy. The point was to observe how when we put our essence in the words we use, our communication becomes powerful (filled with passion). We can express words that sound dead, or we can express words that convey enthusiasm. Our essence connects with others. Our essence comes out whether we want it or not. I live by a definition I heard many years ago. Enthusiasm means God Within. You can also say, Force within, Power within, Spirit within. Whatever resonates with you.

What do you believe your essence to be? Is it one with radiance? Is it one with magnificence? Is it one with joy? Is it one with abundance? Ask yourself every morning as you wake up. How you decide your essence to be for the day will show up regardless of circumstance and regardless of what happens that day.

Remember: you can say it loud or write it down.

Love Thy Neighbor as Thyself

As we love others we actually love ourselves. Even if it is for this "selfish" intention, I choose to take this axiom to heart. The I in you is the I in me. This was one of the principles Jesus Christ, and many other enlightened Masters, has taught us. What results from hurting someone? The hurt comes back to us almost immediately. It is the Law of Compensation in action. It is the demonstration that we are all in this together; the one and the other are the same. This is the ultimate sign of unconditional love. This is Wealth. In our communication with others we can choose to speak words of life or words of death, which in turn will come back to us at the same speed they are uttered.

The more awakened we are to this truth, the more conscious we become with our words. We might begin by first recognizing when we say things that do not build others. Upon this recognition, we began consciously watching the words we use. As we get into this habit, our inner attitude and communication habits begin to change, and ultimately, it becomes natural that we only speak words that build, encourage, uplift, and assist others on their path to Wealth and Freedom.

During the Training Programs my clients participate in, I've noticed that once participants accept the fact that, *"What we say to others we are actually saying to ourselves"*, almost by magic, this awareness causes them to stop and evaluate the words they use. I often explain that our human brain is an amazing apparatus. Once we *accept* a command, it will show us when a command is not aligned with what it was originally set to do.

When you begin stopping your incongruence, you are on your way to your awakening. To what? To moving from being on automatic to being at a higher level of consciousness and awareness. This is the road we want to take and follow.

Wealth in Every Way

Look around. There is abundance of joy, peace, love, greatness, gratitude, beauty, and the list could go on. It is our job to open our heart and see, and claim, and experience the abundance and wealth that surrounds us. What we focus on is that which shows up in our daily lives. Focus on wealth and wealth will manifest. It is the law. Be consistent with your focus and it will not deter you. To maintain your focus, use the sharpest tool you know of – your words. The beauty of all of this is that all of us, with no exceptions, have the same access to this wealth. Why? We are all the same. We were created the same. No one was born with a specific privilege, according to the creator. All of us were given the power to create with our tongue (our words).

I remember the time I was having a conversation with a highly 'successful' business client. He was arguing with me the fact that all of this talking about the power of our words, and how we attract not what we want but who we are, and all this non-sense talk, was just a waste of time. Of course, I didn't argue back to him (that's not the way to connect; in fact, it is a way to disconnect, and that is not what we want in communication.) To understand the place he was at, I began by *finding* a *common ground*. I knew he would get very excited talking about his business, so I asked him, "Tell me Jeff, what brought you success in business?"

Immediately he re-arranged the way he was sitting. His eyes began to shine. He put a smile on his face, and began relating to me the story of his success. I became enchanted by his enthusiasm and the energy he was exerting as he was talking about his meager beginnings, his overcoming of so many obstacles, and finally the reaching of his success. I didn't blink during his twenty minute story. I was hooked heart to heart. I was mesmerized by the tenacity of this man and the potentiality of the human spirit.

When he finished his story about his business, I asked him about his relationships. "Ah. That's a different story," he said. "Do you want to hear about this?" he asked me. And being his coach, of course, I needed to hear. How else was I going to be able to help him see where he was having a breakdown? When he began talking about his most precious relationship, his eyes showed sadness and disappointment, and the words he was using were not words of enthusiasm or joy. Instead, they were words of fear, disappointment and frustration.

At this point, I said, "Jeff, what's the difference between the words you used to describe your business and the words you're using to describe your relationship?"

He stopped abruptly and looked straight into my eyes. "What are you trying to say?" he surprisingly said to me.

"Jeff, what is the difference between the words?" I repeated the same question again, in a quieter way.

"I see what you're trying to do," he said to me. "You're trying to make me look at the words I'm using".

"Absolutely," I responded. Doesn't it sound as if your relationship conveys a different energy, than the energy you conveyed when you were talking about your business?" I asked him.

"I got it now!" was his response. "Then, how could I then change my relationship?" he was quick to ask me.

"How about you begin by changing the WORDS you use to describe your relationship. There is power in the words you use. If you don't believe it yet, I encourage you to do what you did for your business. Go into the unknown. Experiment with the new. Take a risk. Try it for fourteen days, and see the difference, and come back and let me know how it went."

The third week after our first meeting, he called me and left me a message saying he wanted to see me as soon as possible. I could hear the excitement and enthusiasm in his voice, so I knew right of way that he had good news to tell me. He became a believer (of the power of words). The rest is history.

Yes, there is wealth everywhere when we open up to receive it. It comes from the strangest and most unexpected places sometimes; or from the obvious that we can easily miss. It is our job to be open 24/7.

But You Speak Different Words

In a room filled with people who speak different languages, it is possible to have the most outstanding connection. When a connection emerges is as a result of sharing from the deepest part of our essence. At this level, regardless of the words anybody speaks, we are all the same. The fears, the dreams, the passion, the trust, the desires, the ambitions, the singing of our hearts, all in harmony, become one and the same, just because the opening comes from the deepest place where we're all one.

It is amazing to see how in some of my classes, a first day of class where participants are afraid of being strangers in a new land, of not knowing anyone, and even a bigger fear of speaking different languages with little ability to communicate in a common way, can end up, after two and a half hours, feeling connected.

The way to establish a heart connection in a short period of time is to have others talk about their dreams, fears, desires, goals, and visions. How so? Regardless of where you come from, what culture you were raised in, what language you speak, what color your skin is, each of us have dreams, desires, goals, a vision. We might not have them clear in our minds, and we might not be able to express them easily, but all of us have them deep in our heart. We also have fears and doubts. Some of you might say at this point, "I don't," and that's ok.

The awareness I'm bringing to light (consciousness) is that we are all the same, deep down. When we realize this truth, we can see others as they really are. We can look at others as our mirrors. We can go beyond the different languages. We can use words and the energy they convey to connect with others.

Be Aware of the Different Levels of Communication – *noted on previous speech*

Level 1 - a superficial "Hello, how are you?" asked with no intention to bring the conversation to a deep connection.

Level 2 - facts such as "the price of oil is going up".

Level 3 - talk about interests, likes and dislikes, not any deeper.

Level 4 - intimate talk about dreams, aspirations, fears, doubts, purpose.

Steps to a Heart Connection with others - Heart to heart communication

- Be ready to suspend your judgments, advice given, desire to fix, desire to be right.

- Start by sharing a bit of yourself so that the person feels safe sharing from his or her side.

- Take a short time to do this, since the idea is to connect, not to tell your life story to the other who might not be prepared to listen.

- As you go deeper, take the opportunity to ask about their dreams, desires, what they're looking for in life.

- When you are listening, you are listening with your mind, heart, and spirit.

- Ask questions to clarify and have a better understanding.

- Thank the person for their interaction and their openness.

I find that being appreciative of other's openness brings joy and connection. After all, this person is showing trust in you.

For Your Words Only!

Count your blessings, count your words. They are like pearls in the ocean, like the rays of sun, like the wings of a bird, and like you and I when we talk.

Many of you perhaps are familiar with the lyrics, "For your eyes only, only for you, you see what no one else can see, and now I'm breaking free." How about for Your Words Only. "I'll **say** what no one else can say, and now I am breaking **Free!**" Freedom is in the power of your tongue. Freedom is in the power of your Words.

Do you want to be Wealthy? To Be Free? Nothing I give you will bring true Wealth or free from fear, doubt, anxiety, or worry. You (yourself) have the power to create and you have to apply this power. Going a bit further, the power I'm talking about, is the same power that raised Jesus Christ from the death. I choose to call it a Spiritual Power manifested through the Words we speak.

You have the power to create joy, abundance, harmony, and peace with your own tool, with the sharpest of all, your Words. Get excited to know this and apply it in your life. The truth shall set you Free. Become Free, become Wealthy. It takes place in the Now, by speaking and claiming with the words you speak: "I am Wealthy," "I am born Wealthy".

For Parents Only

We as parents have the responsibility of putting words of Life into our children's minds. We are the molders of our children's self-esteem, confidence, trust, respect. We have in our hands a blank canvass to paint, either a spectacular rainbow, or a single line. It is our choice.

A child's young mind is like a vessel that can be filled with words of courage, words of hope, words of love and peace; or words of fear, rejection, anxiety.

What would it take for us as parents to become impeccable with our words?

Children take things literally. When they're little, they have little capacity to differentiate the use of words. I said to my little grandchild (3 years old), "<u>You are</u> a genius." "No I'm not," was her response. "Yes you are," was mine. "No, I'm not," she responded again. I decided to ask her: "Baby, why are you not genius?" "Because <u>I am </u>Amalia." She couldn't disassociate the grammatical use of the words. She hears and takes things literally. This is what I mean by being impeccable with our words. Children store words as they hear them, and those same words become the data that they draw from at a later age.

What do we want our children to speak into existence? What do we want our children to create with their words? What do we want our children to have as their basis for their confidence, self-esteem, trust, and beliefs?

When we become conscious of our power as parents and our obligation to mold the lives of young minds with the words we use, we then understand the tool that is in our hands and its empowering function. Why are we often careful with the words we speak at a funeral? Why do we take the time to reflect in what we say to someone who is hurting? Why do we use words of compassion with a person who is sick? We must do the same when we are talking to children. Envision their little mind as fresh new soil and our words as the seeds we put into this new soil. What would we like to see growing from it? Your words are the seeds! You will only see the fruit in years to come. What kind of fruit would you like to see? What kinds of words do you speak into your child's heart and spirit?

I dedicated this book to my son for the sole purpose of asking him for forgiveness for the words that I spoke to him as a child, and most importantly, so that he will only speak words of life to his children.

For an empowering Program for Parents on "Communication that Builds Confident Children" go to www.thesharpesttooltowealth.com

For Teachers Only

> - Words are the teacher's main *tool.*
>
> - Teachers speak to more ears than others do.
>
> - Because of their position, some people will take their words
>   and live by them.

I've always taught adults, and in my position as a teacher, I've found out that we have the power to give hope and inspire even the most frustrated student. It only takes one or two words of life spoken into someone's heart for them to change, to see light, to find the way. One of the most impacting movies I've ever watched was "October Sky" where the teacher helped one of her students follow his dream by telling him that he *could be anything he wanted if he worked hard enough.* In my view, these were words of hope and life transformed the student's life.

Because of the position teachers often hold, they have certain kind of power to help students succeed or fail in life; to believe in themselves or live a life of unworthiness; for students to live a life of Wealth or life of Poverty.

It is common that some people will attribute their success or failure either to their parents or to a certain teacher who spoke words of hope, encouragement, and optimism into their lives—I'm not referring only to teachers at school but at any level of authority.

Chapter Eight
The Structures and Their Powers

Can We Brake the Cycle?

Some of us have been raised under a structure that stifles creativity, freedom of thoughts, courage, and instills fear, obedience, and submission. Strong hierarchical structures impart power from the top creating, most of the time, obedient, submissive followers. How could we even imagine transcending our human limitations when we cannot move unless ordered by someone with authority? How could we even fathom reaching our potentialities when we need to depend on what others tell us we are? How could we even 'try' to be the person we were created to be when we were never given permission to 'be' it as a child? The good news is that, yes, we can break the cycle and it is up to us. We have the tool.

How Does the 'Opposite' Benefit Humanity?

The opposite to the hierarchical structure—one of openness, transparency, collaboration, trust, listening, asking, involving--creates human beings who will recognize their strengths as well as their limitations and embrace both. And even better, these people will know that if there is a desire to transcend limitations, it is up to them, no one else. There is no blame or guilt because the principles of 'owning your own actions' have been taught at an early age; the principles of having a 'choice' to make your own decisions and 'choosing' have been explained earlier in their development.

When you grow up in a system that respects your individuality, believes in your genius abilities, even at an early age, and teaches you the power of Choice, there won't be questions of self-worthiness during adulthood. How could there be? You, yourself, made many of the decisions that led to your present life. This does not discount gaining support, or counseling from others. In fact, people who are raised under this type of system are more open and free to look for help and assistance because there is no shame involved in asking for collaboration and asking for support when it comes out of your own decision and desire.

What Is the Danger?

In the authoritarian type of structure, it is easy to comply with the belief that Wealth is something that is accessible only to certain people. Who? Those who have the power, or are in power already—in order to get to the Wealth, you either ride in that wave or you're out of it. That is why is common to hear the expression, "You can't create wealth if you don't have wealth". How ridiculous! Where is the power of the human spirit in all of this? On the other hand, the flatter societal structure, where the levels of authority are minimized in order to create individual responsibility, if taken to an extreme, it could create situations where decisions are delayed significantly as a result of processes that are time consuming, such as reaching consensus. But we're talking about Words and Wealth in this book. How does all of this relate to this subject?

Should We Break From It?

If you are one who comes from the hierarchical society or would like to learn how it feels to be raised under this kind of system, and break from it. If this topic does not apply to you or interests you, go ahead and jump to the next chapter.

What Kind of People Does the Hierarchical System Build?

The reason this topic is included in this book is that developing the freedom to create our Wealth with our Words takes a lot of courage and boldness. In my own experience, the hierarchical authoritarian model does not encourage these virtues. To the contrary, it encourages obedience, dependency, and fear.

New Approach

What if we explore what's in the deepest place of a person? What if we take the time to find out what makes others tick? What if we recognize the uniqueness and genius of each human being? What can emerge from this exploration? Many things, and perhaps things that can surprise us when we're not ready for it. The possibilities are unlimited, but perhaps we are not ready to explore the unknown for fear of finding out what's out there. Perhaps we are more comfortable with the known than with the unknown. Perhaps it is easier to follow instructions than to come up with new ways of doing things. Perhaps it is more appreciated when we look up to someone than when we take charge and cross borders. Of course, you will see now how I might be talking from my own perspective.

Freedom-Like Structures

When we have the freedom to choose and are responsible for those choices, we are free; in other Words, we are Wealthy. Through my teachings, I've experienced a large number of people from other countries, aside from North-America, who don't understand what 'freedom to choose' really means. Their wives, husbands, education, lifestyle, etc., have been chosen by their parents and grand-parents. I've also experienced that they are comfortable with this system, and even like it, until they discover the other side of the coin—When we are aware of our choices, we desire Self-leadership, also referred to as Personal Leadership. This doesn't mean that we are getting away from recognizing the Power of the Great Spirit that was placed within us. In fact, is about accessing that Power to lead a life of True Wealth.

Language of Leadership

Leadership begins with our *personal* leadership. Ultimately, who we need to lead is ourselves so that others follow our example by choice. Moreover, to be an exceptional leader, one needs to be an exceptional follower, in terms of humbling ourselves to learn from others. The old leadership structure by position and power is being dismantled as we speak. The new generation is tired of being told what to do and instead are demanding respect and consideration for their opinions and ideas, gifts and talents.

I have been working on dismantling the ins and outs of the hierarchical system. I am openly talking about this so that change comes about. I was affected by this authoritarian style of leadership and did not like the results that produced.

For one, it produces children who become robots. Their only job is to obey blindly and do what everyone tells them, often fearful of using their own creativity and initiative. How could this little human being even venture to do something different when the response is to get punished? This type of behavior gets carried into adulthood. Dependency on others is the only response to survival. Adults become amazing followers with little or no ability to think or create on their own.

The moment we wake up to the reality that we are responsible for our own choices, actions, results, and words we use, thoughts we think, life we live, we are on our way to owning Leadership.

What does it mean to be a Leader and what makes a Leader in our new society? The qualities of empowered leaders come from those who ask powerful questions, listen, and respect the ideas and opinions of others to recognizing their weaknesses as well as their strengths. Leaders see the gifts and talents in others. Leaders are aligned with principles of authenticity, integrity and commitment. Leaders know how to lead themselves first before leading others.

Since leadership begins with personal leadership, it is essential that we look at what that entails to reach the state where we can own our own choices and act from a place that is true to ourselves.

The decision to gain personal leadership is a journey that leads us towards our freedom and wealth. When we're still in a state of dependency, need for others' approval, blaming circumstances or outer world, judging others, and non-commitment, we find ourselves far from our personal leadership.

The words we use to describe ourselves and reframe our position are a starting point for any journey, including our journey towards leadership. We can begin affirming what we desire to see in our lives. We can build a vision and write down together a mission and purpose. We can write the values we want to stand by. We can design the actions we are ready to take so as to lead our life in alignment with our true self.

You and the Leader Within You

For many years, a leader was thought of someone who can direct and tell others what to do. This is what is called the old leadership model. The good news is that there is a new leadership model and one based on reverence to our fellow human beings.

The new leadership model is not based on directing and telling but on listening, asking questions, and then directing. As leaders of the new model, we need to be open and transparent, and respectful of cultures, genders, generational differences. We need to not only be concerned about results and tasks, but also about building relationships. We must model accountability and ultimately be passionate about finding what makes others passionate.

'Leader-ship' really means that we need to first know how to lead our own lives in order to lead others. This includes being good followers as well. It is a win-win relationship and one where everyone learns. The times when a leader knew everything and had all the answers is passé. The environment a leader needs to create is one where mistakes, apologizing and shared responsibility are welcomed and appreciated.

As we change one thing in ourselves everything changes. As we change the vocabulary we lead with, our leadership style changes.

First of all, we need to create our new identity. One that says, "We are leaders." In my experience with clients, when I asked some of them if they consider themselves leaders some say No. My questions is, why not? Because I don't have people under me, was the response.

Here is where we want to change our perception. You are responsible for the most important person in your life, "YOU".

At times, it is easier to manage others, or so we think, than to manage ourselves. I personally know some people who are experts in managing other's lives, and when it comes to their own life, it is a disaster. Of course it is easier to look outwards than inwards. Some people are really afraid of discovering their true Self—It is a path, and one we can travel, beginning by changing the Vocabulary we use in our daily lives. One of my clients said to me, "But it is difficult to change." Right of way, I said, "It might be difficult AND possible." This sentence hit him by surprise. He wanted to take a chance and begin the road of using the Sharpest Tool to Wealth = his words.

1. **Awakening the Leader within you takes a decision that will be supported by your words.** First of all, decide 'You are a Leader'. You want to be responsible for the actions, consequences, and results in your life. There is no space for blaming, criticizing, condemning. In fact, you keep your personal energy intact when you don't waste it on the "enemies of wealth"—blaming, condemning, criticizing, and judging. Those functions are all 'other-oriented'. When we are ready to awaken the leader within us, we are ready to look inward and discover our talents, gifts, ambitions, dreams, vision, mission, and purpose. During this process we will also find our weaknesses, shadows and those things we particularly don't love about ourselves. Once we learn that those things we don't like about ourselves are there for a reason, we begin exploring and accepting them, and by doing this, we began shifting. It is easy to shift things around when we know what they are.

I remembered when I was aware that the word 'nothingness' related to who I was (in my perception) deep down in my conditioning, and that was stopping me from becoming the leader I knew I was. When I finally realized that it was the most valuable gift I received, I got free. I even read a book where God is equated to 'nothingness'. Until I brought it into my consciousness it was probably sabotaging my success. How did Words, in this case, create my new World? I have embraced the word Nothingness in such way that I now give speeches on how our perception can be transformed when we look at words differently. Has my life been transformed because I looked at the Dialogues I used in my life? Absolutely.

2. **We lead from who we are.** The leader and the person are one. Many tend to split the act of leadership from the person. The two are intimately connected and if we want to be successful leaders we need to grow more as a person. As we learn to master our own growth and discovery, we begin our path of mastering leadership from the "inside out".

Leadership is not simply something we do
it is an expression of who we are.

"Your vision will become clearer
only when you look into your heart.
Who looks outside dreams,
who looks inside, awakens."
--Carl Jung

Ask yourself the following questions and reflect upon your answers:

- *What kind of leader are you?*

- *What's unique about how you lead? Yourself and others?*

- *What Words do you use to lead yourself and others?* Are they words of encouragement or discouragement? Are they words of optimism or pessimism? Are they words of fear or hope?

- Is there an opportunity for a shift on your personal leadership style?

Begin with inspecting the Words you use to talk to yourself and others. Words carry energy and this energy is what either inspires or discourages You and others. Be conscious of the Dialogues of your Life; they produce your results.

Session III: Talking to God /
Your Higher Self

Chapter Nine
Teach Me Your Words Thee!

How Do I Connect?

A friend of mine one day said to me: *You don't have to connect to God. We are always connected. Just know that the power is with you, beside you, on top of you. If you don't feel it, it is you who is blocking it. It is the same as electricity—It is there all the time, but you only experience it when you plug into it.*

Many people plug into through meditation, others through prayer, some, by offering each act of the day as small or as big as it is, by expressing gratitude, by just being. How do you connect? Find your way and choose, because the more connection you are aware of, the more creativity, joy, peace, love, beauty and prosperity (in other words, Wealth), you get to experience consciously and unconsciously.

If it is prayer you use, there is an abundance of powerful words of wisdom that cut right through the heart. *A word of prayer is a world of aiming.* What we focus on expands. Focus on words of wealth and wealth will expand.

"When you affirm big, believe big and pray big, putting faith into action, big things happen." –
--Dr. Norman Vincent Peale, Author.

Can I Send You a Message?

The lines are open all the time for those who want to send messages – this was written on a hill. What it didn't have was the address to where the message was suppose to be sent. What was this all about? What was the message in this message? Do we always have to have a receiver or can we send messages out to the universe hoping that someone or something will receive it and respond? If this is the case, our messages have to be very clear. We don't know who or what is getting it, and who or what decodes our messages. It's been said many times that the clearer our messages the higher our chances for them receiving a reply. It just happens that at times we might be vague and broad as to what we are asking for, or would like to see materialized; and guess what? That's what we get. Not knowing the details makes it more challenging for us to notice whether we have received our answers or not. Clarity with our Words creates a permanent connection.

Will You Write Back to Me?

Open a book; talk to a stranger; look at the sky; close your eyes; open your hands. All of these can, at a particular time, bring the answers to you. At times we just don't realize that the answers are within us and surrounding us constantly. We are receiving little written notes, only that sometimes they are not physically written, but virtually. It is in our 'paying attention' that we get to discover the messages. Often the writing is on the wall but we miss it because of our preoccupation with life's little distractions.

Journaling – Many have talked about the power of journaling. It is as if it means everyday writing about our feelings, our achievements, our sensations, dreams, what took place during and whatever comes to mind.

Journaling is really our conversation to our higher self, our heart, our spirit. The purpose of doing this kind of exercise is to let our thoughts come out unfiltered, letting our hands write what our thoughts want to convey. This is what I mean when I say,' Writing back to us'. There are moments when I write, and when I get back to the material I wrote, I'm surprised of the content. I couldn't have written this, is my first thought. What I've discovered is that when we sit and allow our Higher Self to write it is really our deepest Spirit what brings the words and prompt us to do the writing. The words are at times inconceivable by my little self and I recognize that there is something bigger than my body and my brain. There is a Power that is connected with the All. The words seem to come from it, are from the collective, the universal, the heavenly perspective. Those words carry harmony, love, compassion, peace, abundance, eternal joy. Every time I experiment with this type of journaling, the results are incredibly amazing.

Exercise:

Grab a journal.

Sit quietly and just begin writing whatever comes to your mind.

At the beginning, it may appear as if nothing is happening.

As you advance, words that you don't even recognize in your vocabulary begin to flow.

Write for 5 minutes and stop.
Look at the Words that come out this exercise.

You could amaze yourself.

There is infinite awareness within yourself that can get out in words (either spoken or written) when you prompt yourself to access that infinite place within yourself.

Chapter Ten
Now We're Talking

If I Can Only Say It!

"Open the gates of my heart, God, so I can love unconditionally; not that I have to be perfect, but that I will love with the purest and most grateful intention" – this was a prayer, one of my students from Ethiopia said daily, that really had a tremendous impact on me. His life was clearly a mirror of his words. Everyday he would come to class filled with gratitude and joy regardless of his challenges, difficulties, or barriers. To him, his focus was on his vision, which he would call upon daily, so that he will not be deterred by outside circumstances. When I met this young man, I knew that it was absolutely true that we can all live above our circumstances when we have the strategies and awareness to do so consistently. In this case, of course, was his belief in the power of the words, in the power of prayer, which kept him going with such clarity and focus.

You Told Me So

Philosophers, theologians and psychologists have written that there is power inherent in our Words. We can prove it by looking at our results. Why is it then that some us don't care to pay attention to this? Is it ignorance or pride? What is it that blocks us from opening our ears to timeless wisdom? Is it because we don't see these truths with our five senses? Some of us are creatures that use reason and logic strictly to direct our lives. It is proven again and again that as we go beyond our five senses and get into the realm of the spirit, the unseen, the unknown, we find the answers to the intricacies of life. It is a mystery at times to see how we keep bumping into the wall when all we have to do is Listen!

I'm Present With You

This axiom is one of Freedom and Wealth. When the kingdom of heaven is within us, everything happens to us for a reason. When we live in the presence of God, what is there to fear? In this presence we speak from our heart. As we speak from our heart, we speak with authenticity. As we speak with authenticity our truth is revealed.

What happens when we squeeze an orange? What comes from it? Not apple juice, not pineapple juice, but orange juice. Similarly it is with the words that come from that place where we experience the Presence of God, of our Being, of our eternal Spirit – Words of Love, Words of Life, Words of Light are uttered with a force that creates unity, harmony, peace, joy, and abundance.

Does God Have a Voice?

Celine Dion said of Andrea Bocelli that *'he had the voice of God'*. But, does God have a voice?

It was about 10 years ago that I met a lady at a church. The connection she had with God was so intimate that she could hear The Voice all the time. In fact, she was considered schizophrenic by some experts when in reality she was experiencing a level of communication that was unrecognized by some.

When the time came for her to demonstrate what was happening, even the audiences she was speaking to were questioning her reasoning. It was then found that this lady could hear the Voice of God with such precision that she began creating audio materials to distribute in her church. Unfortunately she passed away and her family didn't allow her work to be published. I never found out the reason for this decision, all I knew was that having met this woman, my desire to hear God's voice became a priority in my life.

Key to Hearing God's Voice

I was deaf to God's Voice until I received the three keys:

1. *Journaling*

Sit down with a journal and a pen you really like to write with. Begin writing what comes to mind, spontaneously, for a period of time, without stopping, just allowing your thoughts to flow. Some people call it, writing in faith, simply believing it is God who is dictating and writing. Do not edit. When you're finished, go back and read and hear the Voice of God through the Words you wrote.

2. *Pay attention to a flow of spontaneous thoughts, emotions, visions*

Has it ever happened that you were doing something when all of the sudden a *thought* comes to you to call a certain person, or do something you haven't thought about?

Experience indicates that we perceive spirit-level communication as spontaneous thoughts, impressions, and visions. Therefore, when you want to hear from God, tune to spontaneous, chance-encounter thoughts.

3. Become still so you can sense the flow of God's thoughts and emotions within

"Be still and know that I'm here" – Psalm 46. There is a deep inner knowing (spontaneous flow) in our spirits that each of us can experience when we quiet our flesh and our minds. If we are not still, we will sense only our own thoughts. To receive the pure word of God, it is very important that our hearts be properly focused (on God) as we become still, because our focus is the source of the intuitive flow.

Jesus demonstrated the ability of living in constant contact with God, declaring that He did nothing on His own initiative, but only what He **saw the Father doing, and heard the Father saying** (Jn. 5:19,20,30). *What an incredible way to live!*

Is it possible for you to live out of divine initiative? Yes! Use the 3 keys to hear the Voice of God and the eyes of your heart will be open to live the enlightened life.

Language of Love

Should we be speaking any other language? This is a rhetorical question. The language of love needs to be embedded in all of the other languages including the Language of Business. Love refers to the reverence we must have for the other. "I **See**

You" (the theme of Avatar, by James Cameron) is a greeting the Na'vi use when they meet– it is more than a greeting, it is an acknowledgment. Think of how this type of greeting will make you feel. Similarly, the natives of planet Pandora (in Avatar) realize their connection to all things; only, they call it Eywa instead of God. Higher Self is as simple as having these attitudes in any of our encounters with others.

In a conversation I had last April with a pretty empowered male and three other woman, one of the ladies spoke about a lecture she heard regarding men and women, and how women were wired, genetically to be more loving than men. What surprised me about this idea was that the lecturer, from whom she heard such statement, was someone who is supposed to be enlightened. I don't completely disagree that man and woman might be different, what I clarified throughout our conversation was that perhaps was better to talk about the feminine energy vs. the masculine energy not so much women vs. men. Again, it's about the words we use. I happen to know many men who express more of the feminine energy in their interactions than some women I know.

So, this topic of Love and the language of Love, I'd like to consider it universal as oppose of putting it into a box where some have more than others. It is in fact available to all of us equally. It is in us, and some of us have forgotten. Our job, as I understand, is to remember that we are Love, and how else to bring it into consciousness that by using our sharpest Tool? With words, we can focus on whatever we desire. It was my friend Marc, as I mentioned, a quite enlightened young man, who said that as soon as he made compassion his focus, by speaking it into existence with precision, his heart expanded in such way that he actually felt his heart being bigger than his body. His actions began to shift, mysteriously, or shall we say, automatically. Here we can see what takes place when we decide to (1) focus on something specific, (2) name it, and (3) experience extraordinary results.

Session IV: Talking to Money

Chapter Eleven
Building On the Money Word

Why 'Talking to Money'

When I first planned the content of this book, I had in mind a session called Talking About Money. When I initially developed the manuscript I left it out. It was again, when I was at the airport in Denver, on my way to an Author's Boot camp that I decided to include this important session and be very candid about it. This is my chance to share my feelings and strategies with all of you who do not talk about money because you believe it's not spiritual, or do not talk about money because it was never talked about at home as you were growing up, or because you carry a feeling of shame for having been raised in a family where money did not flow easily, or, better yet, you were raised in a family who struggled heavily as there was scarcity of money.

I had my thoughts about talking about money for a long time. There was a time in my life where I received financial education and was learning how to invest, make more money from money, and keep my finances in order. I became very interested in creating my own business; began learning about entrepreneurship and dedicated a number of years learning how to live, not from a salary but from my professional fees. I started a number of businesses, which relatively didn't give me high profits (on paper-money) but gave me the basis for developing the qualities I needed to become a Leader. Although at that time I thought my focus was on money, it was actually not on money but on my desire to grow as a leader; and I did.

When talking about Wealth (not just money), the development of leadership skills has represented amazing wealth in my life. As an international Consultant, my time has been rewarded according to the industry standards. I had to learn how to value my talents and get paid accordingly. I've discovered that how we are compensated for our work indicates our openness to receive money in our lives. In this world, our value is rewarded in many ways, and one way is with money. We can be either closed or opened to receiving large amounts of compensation for our work, our knowledge and our service. Again, it's our choice. When we add value to others, we are compensated richly. The more value we add, the more money we attract. I've heard the saying, "Do you want more money? If so, add more value to people."

And now, into the real money topic—I mean cash.

How did I talk to money in the past? How did I relate to money? How was my relationship with money? When I began to ask these questions, I began to uncover the feelings I had towards myself and money. Suze Orman in her book *Women and Money* says that our relationship with our money is a direct reflection of our relationship with ourselves. I took this to heart and began exploring this statement. When words hit me, I just don't let them hit me. I let them go deeper until they touch my core.

The 8 *Sharpest* Steps to
Understanding and Changing your Relationship with Money

1. Define and describe the word 'Money'.

2. Write down your beliefs towards Money.

3. Look objectively at your money flow. Are those beliefs serving you?

4. Change the Words you use to Describe Money in ways that Serve you **(The Shift).**
5. Feel and experience the energy that the new definitions and words bring to you.

6. Repeat the new words and embrace the new feeling they produced: "money comes to me easily", "I am a money magnet", "I welcome large amounts of money in my life", etc.

7. Pay attention to the new and different Flow of Money into your life.

8. Be Grateful for it. When you appreciate something, it shows up and stays in your life.
      What we resonate with, we attract!

The Process and the Shift

What were some of the barriers I had towards this word called Money? Did I have the old belief that money was dirty or difficult to get? I became so adamant towards being aware of this belief and transforming it that even when my grandchild was counting money a while ago, I made sure she would not think the same. And when she said, "It is dirty" (relating to money), I immediately had her repeat with me, "Money is important," and this was a conversation with a 2 year old. (I know how beliefs are implanted and also how they are removed or transformed.)

For years, I worked with experts in the area of *belief changing and transforming* at a deeper level. I had the feeling that some conditioning and programming were running my life's actions. I immersed in all types of training, discovery, healing, including specific work in the area of 'Values' (what was important to me).

When I heard Dr. Dimartini in one of his conferences say that *unless*, on our list of Values, **Building Wealth** was one of the top 5 values in our lives, we will not be comfortable making, receiving, creating, earning, and attracting high volumes of money, I paid attention.

This brought me back to the time when I met a consultant who specialized strictly on 'Values'. It's been more than 10 years and I don't remember his name, however, I clearly remember one of the exercises he showed our team regarding the way we could be conscious of our priorities (our values), therefore, conscious about our outcomes.

He had a list of values cut out on small pieces of paper. There were more than 40 values divided into different categories. The idea was for us to pick the 5 most important ones and put it in the order we thought it was important to us.

We physically grabbed each little piece and put it in order from the most valued to the least valued. He told us that whatever we assigned as the 5 predominant values, those were the values we will live by, at that specific time.

Excited about taking action on something I had learned already, I cut up 5 pieces of paper, wrote the values I was interested in, and daily began to place the pieces of paper in this particular order:

WEALTH
RESULTS
UNCONDITIONAL LOVE
FOCUS
ORDER

As I continued doing this exercise daily, my wealth consciousness seemed to expand rapidly. The awareness of wealth, including large amounts of money, became apparent to me in a stronger way.

Reminder: If material wealth has not been a personal motivator in your life, think of all the people you could serve with your resources—We can build wealth so that we can impact the world by building schools, giving scholarships, creating businesses, organizations, paying for someone's hospital bills, helping others achieve their dreams, and the list goes on and on.

Getting back to the exercise and the use of WORDS, notice how it's better to write the WORDS (the value) and then place them in the order of priority. Our mind does something with this process and our consciousness is directly affected.

Once our Value of Wealth is set as our #1 (I recommend this), all kinds of new situations begin showing up in our lives. It is as when we buy a new car and all of the sudden we begin noticing that same car on the road. Why? That car is in our awareness now. Similarly, when we are consciously aware of our most important value(s), the situations that we encounter will remind us of what's most important to us. You will see what I mean when you do this exercise.

Steps to Talking to Money:

- Set Wealth as your priority #1 – this will include the physical aspect of wealth.

- Every time you receive money (pay check, bonus, gift, income), express gratitude

- Carry large bills in your wallet, and from time to time, look at them and be thankful for their energy of abundance.

- Affirm early in morning, and set the intention that "Today is the Wealthiest Day of my Life". Use these words with conviction.

- Just before falling asleep, affirm – I create with ease new and profitable ways of building wealth.

As a result of your new consciousness, money issues resolve and the door to your money abundance opens up in a brilliant way.

As with any energy, we attract not what we want but who we are. We first need the energy and consciousness, which we can create with our WORDS, and then manifestation takes place just in front of your eyes.

> Change begins with the WORDS we use.
> Use your Words as the Tool to Design your New Identity

The Power of Words

"I knew a man who had lost the use of both eyes. He was called a 'blind man'.

He could also be called an expert typist, a conscientious worker, a good student, a careful listener, a man who wanted a job.

But he couldn't get a job in the department store order room where employees sat and typed orders which came over the phone. The personnel man was impatient to get the interview over. 'But you are a blind man', he kept saying, and one could almost feel his silent assumption that his inadequacy in one aspect made the man incapable in every other.

So blinded by the label was the interviewer that he could not be persuaded to look beyond it."

Words have the power to free us or imprison us.

The way we label an individual or thing largely determines our attitudes and reaction towards it, thus the importance of consciously choosing our words.

Final Words:
Your Words Create Your Life

You can claim health, riches, freedom, safety and whatever you want in your life in a deliberate and practical manner. The power is in your Words. Speak of the non-existent things as if they already exist. You do not have to *see* it to know that you *possess* it. To receive the answer, accept it as already done. Call those things that are not as though they were, before the natural eye can see them.

I began this book by talking about conditioning and how our mind (little mind) is programmed by our parents, teachers, culture, surroundings, books, media, etc. I asserted that we often speak out of this conditioning.

The Promise: When We Change the Dialogues of our Life we Discover our Wealth Switch

The use of your "Words as a *Tool* to create your Wealth" is an attitude and a skill. To develop a skill, we need an actual setting in which to practice and some tangible techniques with which to practice. Once we gain fluency in the use of the tool, we develop the attitude, and with it, the lifestyle.

Available Programs Offline and Online

Coaching sessions - 8 weeks

2 Teleseminars per week (45 min. + Q&A)

For more information go to www.thesharpesttooltowealth.com

CPSIA information can be obtained at www.ICGtesting.com
234857LV00004B/1/P